Disconnecting with Social Networking Sites

Disconnecting with Social Networking Sites

Ben Light

Queensland University of Technology, Australia

First published 2014 by
PALGRAVE MACMILLAN

Palgrave Macmillan in the UK is an imprint of Macmillan Publishers Limited, registered in England, company number 785998, of Houndmills, Basingstoke, Hampshire RG21 6XS.

Palgrave Macmillan in the US is a division of St Martin's Press LLC, 175 Fifth Avenue, New York, NY 10010.

Palgrave Macmillan is the global academic imprint of the above companies and has companies and representatives throughout the world.

Palgrave® and Macmillan® are registered trademarks in the United States, the United Kingdom, Europe and other countries.

ISBN 978–1–137–02246–2

A catalogue record for this book is available from the British Library.

Library of Congress Cataloging-in-Publication Data
Light, Ben.
  Disconnecting with social networking sites / Ben Light.
    pages   cm
  Summary: "Ben Light puts forward an alternative way of thinking about how we engage with social networking sites, going beyond the emphasis upon connectivity that has been associated with research in the area to date. Analysing our engagements and disengagements with social networking sites in public (in cafes and at bus stops), at work (at desks, photocopiers and whilst cleaning), in our personal lives (where we cull friends and gossip on backchannels) and as related to our health and wellbeing (where we restrict our updates), he emphasizes the importance disconnection instead of connection. The book, therefore, produces a of theory of disconnective practice. This theory requires our attention to geographies of disconnection that include relations with a site, within a site, between sites and between sites and a physical world. Light argues that diversity in the exercise of power is crucial to understanding disconnective practice where social networking sites are concerned, and he suggests that the ethics of disconnection may also require interrogation" — Provided by publisher.
  ISBN 978–1–137–02246–2 (hardback)
  1. Online social networks.   I. Title.
  HM742.L54 2014
  302.30285—dc23   2014024354

Transferred to Digital Printing in 2014

Contents

Tables and Figures

Tables

Figure

Acknowledgements

This book is a collaborative effort in the sense that my ideas are irrevocably situated amongst the huge body of work already published in this area. It is also a collaborative effort because I have benefited greatly from the input of many friends, colleagues and, of course, the research participants who gave up their time to be interviewed. Naturally, all errors and omissions are mine.

I am deeply grateful to my academic and professional colleagues, past and present, at the University of Salford in the United Kingdom, for their collegiality and for sharing their intellect over the past 15 years. I would also like to recognise the support of my new academic and professional colleagues here at the Queensland University of Technology in Australia. In particular, I thank: Alison Adam, Frances Bell, Gaynor Bagnall, Jean Burgess, Axel Bruns, Elija Cassidy, Colleen Cook, Garry Crawford, Tracie Davies, Victoria Gosling, Nicki Hall, Marie Griffiths, Ben Halligan, Maria Kutar, Alan McKee, Brian McNair, Paula Ormandy, Theresa Sauter, Anne Watson, Patrik Wikström and Darryl Woodford. Thanks also go to the PhD students I have worked with for constantly challenging my ideas. In particular, I would like to express my gratitude to Dr Eileen Wattam for her support with this project and Dr John Effah for allowing me to work with him on the Ghanaian Funerals case study included in this text. I am also very grateful to Felicity Plester and Chris Penfold at Palgrave Macmillan for sticking with me, and this project, to the end.

My sincere thanks also go to the wonderful bunch of people that are the Association of Internet Researchers. In particular, I am indebted to Feona Attwood, Nancy Baym, Kylie Jarrett, Sharif Mowlabocus, Susanna Paasonen, Terri Senft, Jenny Sundén and TL Taylor. I've learned much from you and owe you a great deal in many ways. Thank you for looking after an odd ball who studied Enterprise Systems and who wanted a go at what you do.

Finally, I thank my partner John – who knows when to say the right thing, when not to say anything, and when to provide treats. Not only has John put up with a partner stashed away in a study most weekends during the production of this book, he assisted with interviews and reading badly written drafts. He's all-round good value.

Part I

Appropriating Social Networking Sites

1
The Connectivity Conundrum

Introduction

> Facebook was not originally created to be a company. It was built to accomplish a social mission – to make the world more open and connected.
>
> Mark Zuckerberg, Founder Facebook

The quote above is the opening line of Mark Zuckerberg's letter to potential investors prior to Facebook's flotation on the US stock market in 2012 (see Zuckerberg 2012). In the letter Zuckerberg makes an impassioned plea for the creation of infrastructure [read Facebook] that can facilitate the maximisation of social exchange. The maximisation of the infrastructure he argues is necessary because there is a "huge need and huge opportunity to get everyone in the world connected". Connection above anything else is what should be valued according to Zuckerberg, and he is not alone in this view. But is there such a need? Is there a need for everyone to be connected 24/7? Do we all need a voice on all matters? Do we have to have opinions on everything? Of course we do not and, in practice, connection does not always play out.

This book is about how we disconnect with social networking sites (SNSs). However, I am not simply referring to issues of non-use in relation to those of use. This book is concerned with disconnection as something that we do in conjunction with connection. For example, we might engage in the deletion of relationships in a given SNS but keep others intact or we might use backchannels to create spaces within which we can interact with selected individuals or groups within our broader connected networks. Disconnection is pervasive in our use of SNSs and I argue here for the need to have a nuanced understanding of this. Analyses of disconnection need to go beyond discussions of use and non-use and to encompass understandings of how we make SNSs work for us, or not, on a daily basis in terms of their diversity and mutability. In this opening chapter, I will introduce a way of thinking that seeks to add to our everyday experiences of and with SNSs – a theory of disconnective practice. In short, disconnective practice refers to the potential modes of human and non-human disengagement with the connective attempts made possible with SNSs. These modes of disengagement sit in relationship to our experiences, or not, of a particular site, between and amongst different sites and with regard to these sites and our physical worlds. Such an approach highlights SNSs as operationally contradictory, whereby connection and disconnection are seen to be in play together. In particular, disconnective practice, arguably, acts as a device that allows forms of connection to exist both within and beyond any given SNS.

Over the past ten years, several disciplines have engaged with research regarding SNSs. Particularly within the arts, humanities and social sciences, scholars of communication studies, cultural studies, media and sociology have arguably been at the forefront of such work, alongside others working in business and management studies, information systems, and law. As a result a variety of philosophies, theories and methodologies have been engaged and a diverse range of foci have emerged. Exemplar themes of research include: identity work (boyd 2006, Kendall 2007, Liu 2007b, Livingstone 2008, boyd 2012); friending (boyd 2004, boyd 2006, Donath 2007b, Lampe et al. 2007, Joinson 2008); potential for social capital and relational development (Ellison et al. 2006, Donath 2007b, Ellison et al. 2011); privacy and surveillance (Gross and Acquisti 2005, Ahern et al. 2007b, Donath 2007b, Lampe et al. 2007, Lange 2007, boyd 2008d, Livingstone 2008, Tufekcki 2008, Debatin et al. 2009, Lee 2013); work (DiMicco and David 2007, Clark and Roberts 2010, Smith and Kidder 2010, Brown and Vaughn 2011, Kaupins and Park 2011); celebrity and fandom (Baym 2007, Hutchins and Mikosza 2010, Marwick and boyd 2011b); race (Hargittai 2007b, Barker and Ota 2011, boyd 2012, Hargittai 2012); class (boyd 2012); gender and sexuality (Hargittai 2007b, Light 2007, Light et al. 2008, Jernigan and Mistree 2009, Mowlabocus 2010, Cassidy 2013, Light 2013); and non-users (Hargittai 2007b, Tufekcki 2008). This list is by no means exhaustive, but merely signals the wide-ranging nature of the area. However, it is notable how little research has been undertaken with a nuancing beyond a binary of use/non-use, and particularly whereby notions of disconnection are enrolled.

In the remainder of this chapter, I elaborate on my argument as to the need for a focus on disconnection. To begin I make a brief point regarding how we might historically contextualise SNSs and why it is important to do this beyond the dotcom boom and crash of the early 2000s. I then go on to consider in more detail the extent to which connectivity has been emphasised in SNS research to date, and how we define SNSs. Following this I expand upon how I see disconnective practice and close the chapter by outlining the text overall and how it came into being.

Web 2.0 and the origins of SNSs

It would be very easy for me to recite the usual narrative regarding the emergence of Web 2.0, the participatory turn, social media and SNSs out of the midst of the dot com boom and crash of the early 2000s. This narrative, of course, involves arguments regarding the rationales for the introduction of Web 2.0, Web 2.0's technical and social properties, differences between Web 1.0 and Web 2.0 and stories of the coming into being of various SNS services for instance. Whilst they are interesting, they are not directly relevant to the thesis I want to put forward in this text. I therefore point the reader in the direction of these sources if they wish to follow such matters in detail (O'Reilly 2005, Beer and Burrows 2007, boyd and Ellison 2007, Beer 2009, Burgess and Green 2009, Everitt and Mills 2009, Song 2010, Lovnik 2011, Lievrouw 2012, Lee 2013, Murthy 2013). Instead, what I want to briefly emphasise is the existence of thought around some of the issues that have been brought to the fore since the emergence of SNSs and how these have been presented by some as discontinuities. The discontinuities presented in relation to SNSs are theoretical and empirical in nature and it is important to acknowledge them. I fear pronouncements about the newness of SNSs and their life changing affects sometimes do not account for an appropriate history of technological development in favour of a good dollop of technological determinism.

Let us take YouTube as an example to begin with. It has been argued that YouTube is not like watching television (Tolson 2010). Of course in some ways, YouTube is not like watching television – whatever your conception of television is, be it historical or contemporary. However, YouTube also *is* like watching television – one only has to think of public access programming developed in the late 1960s in America and indeed the contemporary potentials for narrow casting and on-demand services common in much of the developed world. People even use YouTube to watch television programmes in the same way as they would watch television. Apps within smart TVs and games consoles even allow easy access to watch YouTube "television style", on a television. YouTube's original "broadcast yourself" philosophy also tapped into narratives of reality television and minor celebrity, and indeed the practice of Webcamming, whose aesthetics have of course been informed and formed by pornography. YouTube's roots are intimately and irrevocably connected with prior and extant media.

Twitter is similarly situated in relation to an extended web of developments. For example, as has been articulated elsewhere, Twitter is part of a history of public short messaging services (Murphy 2013). It shares similarities with short messaging services regarding the need to express a message in a finite number of characters. Short messaging services for instance were developed via a process involving the analysis of postcards and experimentation with typing sentences and questions. Following this process the inventor of short messaging services Friedhelm Hillebrand determined that 160 characters were sufficient to communicate (Milian 2009). Murphy also argues that Twitter developed from earlier media such as text-based gaming in multi-user dungeons (MUDs), instant message services and internet relay chat (IRC). Moreover, Murphy likens Twitter to the telegraph, which was also used to send short messages quickly. Indeed, an article published a few years ago in the UK press highlights the similarities between Twitter and the Notificator, a robot messenger whereby the public could leave a note, for two hours, on a scrolling message board (Benedictus 2010). Murphy also refers to this technology showing its parallels with Twitter, that the messages posted on the Notificator were readily accessed and shared with others, that it incorporated a timeline and that whether the message was read or not was not guaranteed.

As a final example, we can also contextualise Facebook historically. Despite coming into being in 2004, it has been linked with historical practices of enacting a self through writing. As Sauter (2013) argues, people have historically written about themselves and to others to shape their ethics, values, beliefs and understandings. She suggests that Facebook is a tool through which we do this work today, and that whilst we should not overstate the translatability of these older writing practices we should also not underestimate their contemporary influence. Like Twitter, Facebook also references prior technologies. Here one might for instance think of diaries which capture information about birthdays and facilitate the arrangement of events, photo albums and of course online forums which predate SNSs.

Through these three brief examples of YouTube, Twitter and Facebook, it is possible to see the continuities between these, prior and existing arrangements. Indeed others have also made direct links between SNSs and prior arrangements. For example it has been argued that electronic bulletin boards, such as WELL in the San Francisco area, form part of the history of social media (Tierney 2013). These are arbitrary examples, and of course there are other potential links to be made. In the late 1970s, for instance, it was argued that services such as Ceefax and Oracle (UK), the Captains System (Japan), Datavision (Sweden), Telset (Finland) and Vista (Canada) would pave the way for the "wired household". Along with other technologies such as satellite, disks, data and power cabling, televisions would become programmable information and entertainment centres (Carne 1979). Indeed, Carne states that "In principle, a single wideband connection like an optical fibre could link the system with the world" (Carne 1979: 65). There are also older examples, where one might consider the phonograph – like YouTube, users preferred to listen to recordings rather than make their own (Edison 1878) and the telephone – which according to the *New York Times* in 1877 threatened to expose sewing circle gossip, secret society affairs and the sweet cooings of private courtships (Lauer 2012). Doesn't this all resonate with elements of SNSs as we know them today?

In short, the point I am trying to make is that it has long been argued that technology could become integral to our lives and if we look around we can see that SNSs have roots that extend way beyond the dotcom boom and bust of the early 2000s. This is one of my reasons for framing my work against a backdrop of the social shaping of technology (discussed in the next chapter). I agree with Boczkowski and Lievrouw (2008) that the social shaping of technology offers the ability to make crucial connections between particular technological arrangements over time, and the broader world of artefacts and culture. In doing this, it also pushes us towards conceptions of knowledge construction in the feminist tradition which rebuffs individualistic eureka moments over a perspective which recognises and celebrates group effort and the always incompleteness of what we know. In the next few sections of this chapter, I will go on to focus further upon the short history of research we have that is more directly concerned with SNSs, the Internet and its associations with connectivity more generally.

SNSs and connectivity

Since debates about the implications of the Internet for the creation and maintenance of community began to dominate new media studies in the mid-1990s – see (Rheingold 1994, Jones 1995, Ludlow 1996, Wellman and Gulia 1999), much research into digitally mediated networks and communities has emphasised connectivity. In particular one might consider early work which focused on the "micro level" of social networks and the role of the Internet. This work, for instance, examined the nature of social ties, social capital development, relationship maintenance, frequency of contact, intimacy of contact, network size and network span (Wasserman and Faust 1994, Haythornthwaite and Wellman 1998, Haythornthwaite 2000, Hampton and Wellman 2001, Wellman et al. 2001, Haythornthwaite 2002, 2005, Gennaro and Dutton 2007). There are also larger scale theories which focus on connection as related to networks at the societal level. Castells' (1996) network society thesis, for example, focuses on the capacity of information and communications technology (ICT) based connections as key organising structures of our societies – what he describes as the new social morphology. Here the dominant functions of society, its economic, cultural and media processes, are increasingly organised around networks and connectivity (Hassan 2008). Wittel (2001) also illuminates the connective effects of networked sociality, arguing that it is characterised by a combination, rather than a separation of, work and play. In addition, explaining how people and technology are increasingly coming together with online networks has been the idea of convergence – which according to Poole, is one of the most central themes of research around ICTs for the past 20 years (Poole 2009). It has been further argued that the idea of convergence is particularly powerful because it explains how technology, participatory culture and people are coming together with the potential to surmount rigid boundaries amongst producers from consumers (Postigo 2008). Here, the mapping of how the connection and participation implicitly embedded in "convergence culture" (Jenkins 2008), impacts upon various aspects of western societies, and the industries and individuals within them, for example, has been at the crux of such works as Benkler's (2006) *The Wealth of Networks: How Social Production Transforms Markets and Freedom*, and the work of Bruns (2008) on the nature of transitions from production to "produsage". It has even been argued that any challenges to networks need to happen through networks. As Castells (2004) argues, it is characteristic of the network society that the dynamics of domination and resistance rely on network formation.

From within and amongst these discussions, through research focusing on the multitude of ways that we organise ourselves with online networks, various conceptions of networked sociality, including networked individualism (Wellman 2001), networked collectivism (Baym 2007), the networked household (Kennedy and Wellman 2007), networked publics (Ito 2007, boyd 2008c) and networked masculinities (Light 2013) have come into being. While this work may attend to nuanced understandings of digitally mediated sociality, it important not to underestimate how connection and connectivity have become significant areas of emphasis in our definitions of SNSs and in our understandings of how these technologies are used. I believe that our research is focused heavily on the nature, and possible implications of, the connections established with SNSs, over other possible outcomes, as we engage with them. I am in agreement with Mejias (2010) that we may have become nodocentric in our thinking. In taking this view, it is argued that there is a tendency to construct a reality whereby only nodes can see other nodes; it privileges this and in doing so discriminates against the invisible and other – that we might not see because we are looking for nodes – for elements of connectivity. To be clear, I do not think this research is bad or wrong, such research is wholly necessary – connection matters. I also do not think that others ignore that disconnection exists with digital media. What I am arguing for is an additional lens on SNSs which adds to our understandings of such phenomena. Attempting to create some semblance of symmetry requires us to consider the role of disconnection as an active part of our engagements with SNSs. However, to date, and while many acknowledge the futility of technological determinism and the unexpected appropriation of SNSs, I am not convinced we have made disconnection a substantial focus of investigation.

There is a huge amount of research on SNSs available to us now, but if one considers how we define SNSs, the questions often asked, and findings obtained, these generally enrol notions of use and more specifically use as related to an implicit assumption of connection. If we consider how SNSs are defined, connection is integral to this. For example, SNSs have been said to incorporate and articulate a list of other users with whom they share a connection, allowing users to view and traverse their list of connections and those made by others within the space (boyd and Ellison 2007) and that the public display of connections is a crucial component of SNSs (boyd 2006, boyd and Ellison 2007, Ellison and boyd 2013). It has been further suggested that the point of the SNS profile is to establish (and demonstrate) linkages and connections (Miller 2008) and that they are websites explicitly aimed at creating and/or maintaining social relations (Schwarz 2010). Moreover, these connections have the capacity to reach out "beyond" the boundaries of any given space and they are characterised as not being disconnected from other social venues (boyd 2006). To be clear, I agree with the general point boyd is making here: that we have to recognised SNSs as another space we interact with and one which can be intimately interwoven with other parts of our lives. boyd is talking in particular about young people here, but I believe the argument hold for other age groups too. However, we have to be careful not to overstate the lack of disconnection that comes with engaging with SNSs. SNSs may well connect us beyond the Internet and with other social venues. That said, SNSs are engaged as a space in their own right and some people may never connect the relationships they develop in these spaces with those in the physical world. These users may be in the minority, but they do exist.

Connection is also evident in the way that particular SNSs are described and defined in academic study. For example, the point of Twitter has been described as the maintenance of connected presence (Miller 2008) and YouTube as a space where many different cultural flows intersect and "diversely motivated" media producers brush against each other (Jenkins 2009). Connectivity is also emphasised in how those owning or providing SNSs describe them, as shown in Table 1.1.

Table 1.1   SNS descriptions by SNS providers – February 2014

Facebook helps you connect and share with the people in your life.

The ultimate gay social network. Are you looking to meet new friends, find a partner, or just hook-up? **Fitlads** is the place!

Capture and Share the World's Moments **Instagram** is a fast, beautiful and fun way to share your life with friends and family.

Welcome to **LinkedIn**, the world's largest professional network with 250 million members in over 200 countries and territories around the globe. Our mission is simple: connect the world's professionals to make them more productive and successful.

Twitter helps you create and share ideas and information instantly, without barriers. Twitter is the best way to connect with people, express yourself and discover what's happening.

YouTube allows billions of people to discover, watch and share originally created videos. YouTube provides a forum for people to connect, inform, and inspire others across the globe and acts as a distribution platform for original content creators and advertisers large and small.

However, scholars have also been clear to articulate that although SNSs and networked publics might encourage a particular line of appropriation (boyd 2008c, boyd 2011), or attempt to set the tone for use (Papacharissi 2009), they also acknowledge things might not play out as the designer intended. It is clear that users are actively involved in connective practice themselves, beyond what the "programme" says (van Dijck and Poell 2013). I would also add here that these users are also involved with disconnective practice with the programme and beyond what the programme says.

My suggestion is that our research in this area can be network centric and this coupled with SNSs in practice can create an emphasis on connectivity. This emphasis, I argue has the capacity to shape our ontological and epistemological understandings of SNSs and it is necessary to critically engage with this and consider if we need to adjust accordingly. Such a connective emphasis exists, for instance, in relation to work on identity management and the performance of friendship through SNSs, where it is present in discussions of how SNSs are employed to define and verify user identity through group associations (Donath 2007a, Larsen 2007, Liu 2007a, Livingstone 2008, Cover 2012), in considerations of how SNSs alter the nature of friendship itself (boyd 2004a, boyd 2006, Donath 2007a, Lampe et al. 2007, Joinson 2008), in projects emphasising the role of SNSs in social grooming processes (Donath 2007a, Tufekcki 2008) and the development of social capital (Ellison et al. 2007, Ellison et al. 2011), and in discussions of the ways that SNSs bridge "online" and "offline" networks (Subrahmanyam et al. 2004, Lampe et al. 2007, Baym 2010). The capacity of SNSs to bridge and connect – or "collapse" – networks and social contexts (Kendall 2007, Hogan 2010, Marwick and boyd 2011b), means that connectivity can be implicated in discussions of privacy in SNSs, around issues of what gets disclosed in these contexts, to whom and how (Ahern et al. 2007a, boyd 2008a, Livingstone 2008). A connective emphasis is equally present in work on the ways that creative processes are enhanced through SNS-based connection and collaboration (Light et al. 2012); in studies which outline how companies monetise the connections embedded in SNSs, such as Gerlitz and Helmond's (2013) work on the "like economy"; and in observations of the roles of SNSs in contemporary protest culture and social movements (Lindgren and Lundström 2011), where, for example, social media has been described as shifting the focus from collective to connective action (Bennett and Segerberg 2012).

Where matters of disconnection enter into considerations of SNSs head on, it is typically with respect to issues of non-use, and framed within discourses of digital inclusion and the digital divide (Hargittai 2007a, Hargittai 2012), in terms of a general lack of interest in SNS activity (Tufekcki 2008, Portwood-Stacer 2013) or matrices of shades of use in comparison to heavy use (Hargittai and Hsieh 2011). While such work is valid and important, through its emphasis on haves and have-nots, users and non-users, it nevertheless establishes ideas of disconnection within SNSs in dichotomous ways and on very particular terms. Disconnection tends to be raised beyond these themes only in passing, or is implied. For example, Baym (2007) in her study of online fandom points to the use of SNSs in fragmented ways across multiple sites which helpfully points, implicitly, to notions of disconnection, and Crawford (2009) in her work on disciplines of listening engages not only with discourses of connection through listening, but also disconnection via her attention to acts of not listening. Cassidy's (2013) work on participatory reluctance – the engagement with SNSs reluctantly is also worth mention here, as is Papacharissi's (2010, 2011) work regarding private spheres of interaction, particularly her commentary on the creation of privée spaces and our abilities in respect of redactional acumen. A final piece of work of interest here is that regarding conceptions of forgetting in digitally mediated environments, where Mayer-Schönberger (2011) discusses potential responses to digital remembering, particularly in terms of digital abstention. However, whilst all this work touches on disconnection, I think it is fair to say it is not the focus of attention throughout. An exception, and very late addition to this text, which I have only been able to acknowledge briefly as I came upon it as this text was in production, is the work of Terro Karppi. This body of work is directly concerned with disconnection in terms of the modes and practices associated with digital suicide, trolling, lurking and leaving Facebook (Karppi 2011; 2013; 2014). I am in agreement with Karppi that disconnection is a necessity in SNSs and social media environments more generally and encourage readers to explore his work further.

My task here then, is to depart from the existing general tone of discussions regarding SNSs and look for other engagements with these arrangements that further nuance our understandings of the appropriation of SNSs.

Defining SNSs

In broad terms, social networking involves social relations amongst people who have (and indeed desire) some type of relationship or affiliation. Therefore, sets of social networking sociotechnical arrangements are often conceptualised as providing support for such activities. Prior arrangements such as chat rooms, mobile phones and landline telephones all hold and continue to hold the potential to facilitate social networking. We consequently have to acknowledge that contemporary SNSs, and the study of these, is historically situated. There may be new challenges raised, but there is also continuity. For most people, new media contribute to, rather than permanently dislodge, social and other routines (Wellman 1996). That said, a set of arrangements have emerged around which there is some agreement regarding the characteristics that define them as "social network sites" or "social networking sites". Arguably, much of this agreement coalesces around the definition put forward by the danah boyd and Nicole Ellison in their editorial to the special issue of the *Journal of Computer Mediated Communication* on SNSs (boyd and Ellison 2007). This definition is primarily based on the use of the term "network" rather than "networking" because, they argue, social network sites generally are not concerned with the initiation of new connections and rather their distinguishing feature, compared to other forms of computer-mediated communication, is that they display a social network. On this basis, boyd and Ellison put forward the following definition:

> We define social network sites as web-based services that allow individuals to (1) construct a public or semi-public profile within a bounded system, (2) articulate a list of other users with whom they share a connection, and (3) view and traverse their list of connections and those made by others within the system. The nature and nomenclature of these connections may vary from site to site.
>
> (boyd and Ellison 2007: 211)

In response David Beer has critiqued this definition, arguing it is too broad and has limited analytical value (Beer 2008). Beer prefers the term "social networking site" as this narrows down matters to applications where networking is the main preoccupation. Further, he states that:

> It seems to me, reflecting on the story so far presented by boyd and Ellison that this is a real danger. Capitalism is there, present, particularly in the history, but it is at risk of looming as a black box in understandings of SNS.... So, when we ask about who are using SNS and for what purpose, we should not just think about those with profiles, we should also be thinking about capitalist interests, of third parties using the data, of the organizing power of algorithms (Lash

2007a), of the welfare issues of privacy made public, of the motives and agendas of those that construct these technologies in the common rhetoric of the day, and, finally, of the way that information is taken out of the system to inform about the users, or, in short, how SNS can be understood as archives of the everyday that represent vast and rich source of transactional data about a vast population of users.

(Beer 2008: 526)

Ellison and boyd (2013) have maintained their position regarding the term "social network site", but have recently revised their definition further arguing that, at the time of writing the landscape called for this. Their current definition is:

A social network site is a networked communication platform in which participants 1) have uniquely identifiable profiles that consist of user-supplied content, content provided by other users, and/or system-level data; 2) can publicly articulate connections that can be viewed and traversed by others; and 3) can consume, produce, and/or interact with streams of user-generated content provided by their connections on site.

(Ellison and boyd 2013: 158)

Before I engage with this further, I want to present some data from the study regarding how my participants defined SNSs. During the interviews participants were asked to name the SNSs they were aware of and these are listed in Table 1.2. Not all the sites listed in this table are mentioned again in the book, as participants, although being aware of certain sites did not use them. Participants were also asked how they defined SNSs and each implied some form of connection-making ability within their definition. However, embedded in their definitions was much more information about what they thought SNSs did. The participants defined SNSs as a thing done. SNSs came into being through

Table 1.2   SNSs as mentioned by study participants

Face Party, Facebook, Fitlads, Flickr, Friends Reunited, Gaydar, Google+, Grindr, Grono, Hi5, Imgur, Instagram. Bebo, Kick, LinkedIn, Mixi, MyClass, MySpace, Nasza-Klasa, Picassa, Pinterest, Reddit, Skype, Soundcloud, Spotify, Tumblr, Twitter, Whatsapp, YouTube that they produced. Here, for example, SNSs were defined by their abilities to enable: sharing of opinions; sharing of content – music, photos, videos; being nosey; meeting up for sex; self promotion; commercial marketing; access to entertainment and messaging. In defining SNSs, participants also compared SNSs with each other. For example, Jacob defined Linked In as "Facebook for grown ups", Daphne compared Facebook with Twitter in terms of the kinds of information she saw as possible for sharing in each space, Hannah said that Instagram was like a watered-down version of Facebook and Bob talked about Twitter being more complicated to navigate than Facebook, yet having less functionality. SNSs were also defined in relation to other sets of arrangements: Jenny compared Linked In with an online curriculum vitae and business card; Jyoti said they were like MSN messenger or Yahoo messenger, and Katie pointed to the pervasiveness of SNSs features in other sites such as news media – indeed Kevin cited the UK's Daily Mail newspaper as an SNS "because so many people have profiles and they comment and they discuss every article and they have forums building into it".

A further line of discussion pointed to the use of SNSs that challenges us to think about how we currently define SNSs; where SNSs are not used for networking or displaying network information. Here for instance, people talked of using YouTube without having an account, engaging with it as a device to access entertainment, such as TV programming, films and user-generated comedy or educational content such as how to undertake DIY around the house, fix cars or learn about a topic for a course they were enrolled in. Twitter was sometimes used in this way too, as a read-only medium in relation to such areas as news, work and celebrity for instance. Although such following produced a social network of sorts, the participants who spoke of using Twitter in this way reported not tweeting themselves. They had an account only so they could access the content of others. They completed the minimum of fields required to generate an account and did not accept followers (as they put it, what was the point, they didn't tweet). Facebook was talked of in similar terms; people had accounts to read other people's content or play games. Facebook was cited several times as a gaming platform. In this mode, Facebook was not used to interact with others and such users, like those operating similarly via Twitter, participants spoke of not posting content themselves on their own wall or on that of others. These participants' walls were also locked so no one could post content on them. Spotify was also mentioned here. Even though Spotify has SNS functionality, several participants reported using it solely as a music streaming service as they did not want others to access their activities (usually for reasons of embarrassment as I discuss later in the book). The points made by my participants resonate strongly with the extant literatures which question the extent of the centrality of the profile in favour, for instance, of news feed type functionality (Lange 2007, Albrechtslund 2012) and the use of SNSs as merely archives of relationships (Richardson and Hessey 2009).

A final line of discussion regarding defining SNSs, related to what participants did not see as an SNS. Here the most common responses included reference to sites that were seen as informational such as the Google search engine, Wikipedia, government websites or those where one could purchase products and services, such as Amazon and eBay. However, this discussion also raised contradictions amongst participants as other things that had been defined by some as SNSs, where not classed as SNSs by others. Here for instance the UK's Daily Mail site, was not seen as an SNS by Simon as it was seen as purely an informational site and even though others had emphasised the social networking capabilities of sites such as Gaydar, Kevin felt that dating-type sites did not count as they were "just a transaction".

What we see in my participants' responses is a diversity of opinion as to what constitutes an SNS. However, in many ways, their comments resonate with boyd and Ellison's definitions. Indeed we can see the participants struggle as much as academics do in pin pointing what SNSs are. In the end, we are left with trying to understand them via what they do. This is somewhat my point of departure with Ellison and boyd. I do not see adopting the term "social *networking* site" as only allowing for a focus on those which are implicated in the seeking of new connections, rather than social *network* site, which is associated with a focus on connections already made and the public display of those connections. For me, the term "social network site" not only misses the role of SNSs in allowing for new connections to be made, it also underplays the fact that, for most people, these sites require ongoing networking activity amongst people who already know each other in order to keep them working. Moreover, it is notable that in the 2013 Oxford Internet Survey of Britain respondents reported that the most common way to meet new people online was with SNSs (Dutton et al. 2013). I therefore prefer the term "social networking sites", like David Beer, because I like to be reminded that these things are never complete. SNSs are brought into being by constant networking activity. In addition to this, I find it difficult to shake out of my head the potential of multiple interpretations of SNSs and their malleability. This is evident in my participants' responses, in this chapter and also throughout this text. SNSs are more than the features and functions they are inscribed with – they are, for example, sites of politics, modes of profit making, entertainment devices and recruitment devices. I do not have the complete definition of SNSs. I actually do not think it is possible to produce one because they are so mutable and malleable. Instead, I prefer to be clear about the matters I am referring to and be comfortable that other people may have other positions. I therefore see value in boyd and Ellison's work, Beer's critique, particularly his emphasis on SNSs as networking sites as loaded with power interests, and my own participants' understandings. I am comfortable engaging with elements of these understandings of SNSs under the very broad definition of SNSs as Internet platforms that encourage user-generated content and exchange, as put forward by Tierney (2013).

Introducing disconnective practice

In the rest of this book, I intend to put forward evidence to support the case for the importance of theorising SNS appropriation in relation to what I term disconnective practice. Disconnective practice, I argue, involves potential modes of disengagement with the connective affordances of SNSs in relationship to a particular site, within a particular site, between and amongst different sites and in relation to the physical world. Disconnective practices involve, and are often embedded in, SNSs users' decisions regarding the extent to which their connection and disconnection through a site or sites will be determined manually or automatically and via human or non-human activity. That is, there is power in disconnective practice in not doing as much as there is power in doing. For example, users might avoid multiple site connection within SNSs simply through eschewing automated upload functions and Facebook like buttons embedded in other sites, or they may attempt to keep their various social realms separate through actively untagging photographs of themselves. Disconnective practice can also involve recontextualisation work, where for instance, the user chooses not to click Facebook like buttons embedded in other contexts and instead manually relocates material from those other contexts into Facebook through the cutting and pasting of URLs. While such practices might be underpinned by concerns about privacy and discretion in SNSs, and by the activities occurring directly within an SNS, I will show how disconnective practices can equally be influenced by users' physical surroundings and the materiality of digital things – for example, sounds at work, the physical arrangement of computer screens, and the availability of mobile phone signals. Perhaps due to the emphasis upon connection, and the pervasiveness of connectivity as an idea associated with SNSs, I illustrate, users do not employ the terms "disconnection" or "disconnectivity" in relation to their use of SNSs. Instead, they talk about their use of what I term disconnective practice in terms of things such as untagging and not linking multiple sites. This short introduction to disconnective practice is placed here to sensitise the reader to the ideas I will develop throughout this text. For those that cannot wait, they will find a full exposition of how I think about disconnective practice in the closing chapter.

Outline of the book

I began researching the Internet in 1999 as a side project to my larger body of work regarding organisational technologies; however, it wasn't until 2006 that I started to engage fully with this area. Since then I have focused my research efforts around the Internet and particularly SNSs where I have studied sites such as Facebook, Gaydar, Habbo Hotel and YouTube. My thinking for this book's material is influenced by this work and is augmented by in-depth interviews with 26 people, of mixed gender, race, sexuality and age, and who reside in the north of England. The daily occupations of participants included, for example, those who were retired on the grounds of ill health, those in manual work such as cleaners, a train driver, school teachers, office workers, a politician and those working in information technology. The interviews focused on how participants engaged with SNSs, but in particular the themes of questioning related to the navigation of multiple spaces of everyday life. Participants were asked about how they understood SNSs, their use of devices and software, modes of connection made, their thoughts on ethics and law, public space usage and usage as related to health, work and play. As my group of interviewees are relatively small, it has not been possible focus upon nuances to my findings regarding socio-demographics and neither did I intend to. I also do not engage with the specific analysis of any given SNS. However, it is perhaps helpful for the reader to know that Facebook and Twitter were the predominant SNSs mentioned as used by my participants. Perhaps unsurprisingly given the study was conducted in the UK in 2013, Facebook was the site most likely to be engaged with. Everyone used YouTube but it did not feature generally as a site people held accounts with, and was treated more as a mechanism for accessing and sharing content via other platforms – often without users having an account. LinkedIn usage was tempered mostly by the employment status of the individual participants as discussed in Chapter 5. A few participants used Fitlads, Flickr, Gaydar, Grindr and Tumblr.

This book does not, and I cannot stress this enough, provide an account of how everyone is using SNSs today. I was, importantly, led by my participants in terms of their lived experiences of SNSs, guiding the interviews only by high level themes rather than being incredibly specific. I do not expect the participants' experiences here to be the account of how SNSs are used, their experiences are engaged to give insight into the possibilities of SNS use and facilitate a theorisation of disconnective practice.

When I first began the study, I was interested in how people navigated multiple spaces given the increasing pervasiveness of different kinds of SNS. I knew, from my previous research, those who engaged in non-mainstream networking (particularly gay men) sometimes kept spaces apart and sometimes these were connected. When I started asking the demographically diverse participants of this study questions about multi-site navigation, a common response was contradictory – I don't connect them, or I do but only in these ways, on these terms, or with these people or things. It became clear to me that people were navigating single and multiple sites via engaging in disconnection and my focus shifted. These discussions led to the accounts of connection and disconnection I draw upon here to put forward a theory of disconnective practice.

Part I of this text, in which this chapter is situated, is concerned with laying out how one might think of SNSs and their appropriation. In Chapter 2, I provide insights into how I am more broadly framing my understanding of the appropriation of SNSs and the role that disconnection plays. Within this chapter, I argue that the Internet, and the applications associated with it, are subject to interpretation by various social groups, with varying agendas. As a consequence of the Internet arrangements being subject to a variety of narrations, it is perhaps most helpful to work with this dialectical position. I also advocate for the interpretation of the Internet as just another space of our everyday life rather than another world. This chapter also lays out the social shaping of technology as a way to understand a hybrid view of technological development and appropriation where we have varying possibilities to shape technology, but we are also shaped by it. I also provide an outline of my conceptions of power, as I see this as integral to notions of connection and disconnection. Chapter 3 pays particular attention to the extent and nature of the engagements we have with things beyond the human in our everyday appropriation of SNSs. Here,

I discuss contexts of appropriation in terms of geography, time and situated use – "the where", "the when" and "the with" of use. I also examine the work of applications and apps, the functions they have, the interfaces they present themselves to us through, the devices we engage with them via and the infrastructures upon which they and we engage. The point of this chapter is to clearly demonstrate how non-human mediators are implicated with us in our use of SNSs, and disconnective practice in particular.

In part II, I emphasise disconnection in relation to publics, which is not to say that the matters contained within part III regarding personal disconnection do not bleed into this arena, and vice versa. Of course they can. The division I make here is one of emphasis. Chapter 4 explores how we might participate with SNSs in the mediation of public life where it goes beyond the boundaries of work and home. Here I consider SNSs in terms of how they and we are implicated in the construction of further public spaces and the extent to which these reflect more general interpretations of decent behaviour. I am interested here, in how disconnective practice is implicated. How is disconnective practice played out in our navigation of public spaces with and within SNSs both in terms of what we do and what we are allowed to do? Chapter 5 focuses upon disconnection as it relates to our engagement with work. A greater number of people are now engaging with SNSs and for many these activities are becoming intertwined with their occupation irrespective of whether they are gainfully employed, engaged in voluntary work, unemployed or retired. This chapter addresses how people navigate SNSs through the enrolment of selective connectivity and more specifically disconnective practice. It highlights disconnective practice as holding potential to be a retrospective act, to be engaged in relation to work talk, as linguistic cover and as related to the nature and structure of a person's role. I also highlight the roles of institutions with respect to disconnection.

Part III emphasises personal levels of disconnection. Chapter 6 concentrates upon how we personalise the use of SNSs by engaging with disconnective practice. This chapter examines how disconnection is present in the navigation of relationships in areas such as gossip, how we deal with boring people and of friend culling, for instance. Disconnective practice is also shown to be integral to identity work where the desire for anonymity and multiple disconnected accounts may play a part. Importantly, this analysis demonstrates how disconnective practice need not be read as resistance, and rather as something positive and necessary that adds value to our engagements with SNSs. This chapter also discusses the role of ethics and judgement in shaping acts of disconnection, drawing upon ideas of editorial ethics and notions of respect for others. It also highlights the sometimes-negotiable nature of disconnection. The affects of agency and structure on the personalisation of use with disconnective practice are considered within this chapter too. This discussion engages with the potentials for disconnection in terms of failures in the affective associations with SNS features, rejections of SNS philosophies, apathy regarding the commercial imperatives of SNSs and the limits of disconnective practice as a mode of commercial resistance. The chapter also reveals that disconnective practice is something that may itself have commercial interest and value. Chapter 7 gives attention to how disconnective practice might figure in peoples' engagements with SNSs as related to health and wellbeing. It considers issues associated with users accessing health information, sharing health information and receiving health information. Through this analysis, psychological elements of disconnective practice are revealed as related to conceptions of how we conceive of SNS space, the content we share in such spaces, the people we are connected with, or not, and the relevance of the things we share or might receive. This chapter also engages with ideas of the materiality of SNSs in health contexts whether this is through formal education programmes, political acts of posting made by those with health conditions and the affects of SNSs on health. The ethical tensions of engaging with SNSs in relation to health are also discussed and two case studies are enrolled to consider culture as a mediator of disconnection.

Part IV contains the conclusions of this study. In Chapter 8 I bring together the various threads of preceding chapters to elaborate on what a theory of disconnective practice might contain. A theory of disconnective practice, I argue, incorporates attention to geographies of disconnection, disconnectors, disconnection modes, disconnective power and the ethics of disconnection.

2
Theorising Technological Appropriation

Introduction

In the opening chapter of this text, I discussed how I thought of SNSs, and how I thought SNSs were being talked about in relation to notions of connectivity and disconnection. In this chapter I want to provide some insight into how I am more broadly framing my understanding of the appropriation of SNSs and the role that disconnection plays. In order to do this, I begin by raising two contextual themes that are relevant to the historical and continued development of the Internet and SNSs. The first theme concerns the potentials for the Internet to enrich our world versus its potential for harm, and the second is the extent to which that activity mediated by the Internet is perceived to have material effect. Following this, I outline some key elements of a way of theorising appropriation, the social shaping of technology, particularly as it relates to understandings of technological development and the characterisation of users. The chapter concludes with a brief note on my thoughts regarding power as I see this as a necessary feature of connection and disconnection.

SNSs are situated within a broader history of argument regarding the Internet's utopian and dystopian properties. For instance, in relation to utopian perspectives, Rheingold's (1994) work signalled a possibility for the reinvigoration of community via the Internet, and others suggested increased instances of everyday communication (Wellman and Gulia 1999, Robinson et al. 2000, Quan-Haase et al. 2002). Other associated positive effects included conceptions of the Internet as enabling fluidity of identity and improved ethical relations regarding trust, care and honesty, leading to claims of social levelling, egalitarianism and a reduction of social exclusion (Dubrovsky et al. 1991, Walther 1992, Turkle 1995, Parks and Roberts 1998, Mele 1999). In contrast, those engaged with the dystopian thesis put forward arguments that the Internet was synonymous with social isolation and ethically dubious behaviour, lacking authenticity and accountability, and was somehow a weaker form of communication than those enacted "face-to-face" (Sproull and Kiesler 1992, McLaughlin et al. 1995, Doheny-Farina 1998, Kraut et al. 1998, Galston 2000). My sense is that for many now engaged with the study of the Internet, such dichotomous arguments are of limited value. We know that the Internet and the applications associated with it, old and new, are subject to interpretation by various social groups, with varying agendas, resulting in a diversity of narrations in this respect. We also know that the influence of the Internet and its applications are variable – they can be good, bad and ugly – often simultaneously. I agree with Fuchs (2011) that although one can distinguish three kinds of SNS research: techno-pessimistic, techno-optimistic and critical/dialectical, the latter offers more helpful insights.

SNSs are also situated within historical and indeed, in some areas, ongoing arguments regarding the extent to which digitally mediated space is seen to be real. Arguments regarding the utopian and dystopian affects of the Internet can often be woven into assertions with respect to the realities of digitally mediated space. Here the Internet can be presented as something other; something disconnected from real life that offers opportunities to do things that could not be done in reality. These things are often given value in terms of being seen as good (identity fluidity/social inclusion) or bad (anti-sociality/reduced sociability). However, even if not stated explicitly, implicitly such arguments are predicated on some kind of material impact upon our lives and can share an underlying agreement that digitally mediated space matters. Indeed, for many the Internet and its associated applications are conceptualised as merely just another space within our social arrangements (Hampton 2004, Carter 2005, Mesch and Talmud 2006, Paasonen 2010). I am in complete agreement with this understanding of the Internet and its applications, as Wittel suggests, the term virtual is misleading in that it suggests a doubling of reality (Wittel 2001). However, it is not just a doubling of reality implied by the use of such a term that makes it problematic. The use of the term virtual also implies a synthetic quality, something that is not real. I therefore do not agree that:

> The cyber-prophets were wrong: there is no evidence that the world is becoming more virtual. Rather the virtual is becoming more real; it wants to penetrate and map out our real lives and social relationships.
>
> (Lovnik 2011: 13)

I disagree because I believe the Internet has always been as real as any other aspects of our realities that we construct – some of us perhaps just did not realise at the time. However, I do agree with Lovnik's point regarding the extent of the importance of the Internet in our lives and I think this has influenced our perceptions regarding the extent to which we enrol notions of the virtual, the online and the offline in our thinking regarding the contemporary Internet. As Baym states:

> To ask whether mediated communication is as good as unmediated interaction, or whether online relationships are as good as mediated relationships, is to miss the point. It is not a question of either/or, of one versus the other. It's a question of who's communicating, for what purposes, in what contexts, and what their expectations are.
>
> (Baym 2010: 153)

My additional concern to Baym's, in this text, is the consideration of who's *not* communicating, for what purposes, in what contexts and what their expectations are. Therefore we need to think of SNSs as another space people choose to inhabit, or not, alongside others in their lives.

Arguments regarding the dystopian and utopian affects of the Internet, and questions regarding its realness are further meshed with questions regarding the extent to which we socially determine it as compared to the extent to which it determines us. Here the point is the extent to which we are able to engage with the Internet and its applications to have them do what we want them to do, in comparison to the extent to which we are being directed to particular ways of living due to the unbridled power of technological progress. I, like many others who study the Internet, take a hybrid view of such matters. In short we have varying possibilities to shape technology, but we are also shaped by it. Indeed this state of affairs is an ontological and epistemological necessity for the thinking regarding disconnective practice I put forward in this text. Disconnective practice, I will demonstrate, involves navigating with sociotechnical arrangements in our attempts to make SNSs work for us. In order to understand this theoretical position further, I will now briefly introduce the body of work known as the social shaping of technology (SST).

The social shaping of technology

SST perspectives emphasise technological appropriation as something involving a range of human and non-human actors. In taking this position, this body of work rejects technologically deterministic accounts of the nature of technology, its development and its use (Sørensen 2002, Latour 2005). By technological determinism, I refer to depictions of technology and change which are purported to be beyond social influence. Technological determinism is prevalent today as Lee makes clear in his recent text on Facebook:

> Every major technological innovation propels humanity forward to the point of no return. Hardly anyone would seriously consider giving up the Internet, cell phones, automobiles, and everyday comfort and convenience. Instead of turning back, we continue to innovate and push humanity towards the next point of no return. It is a good thing.
>
> (Lee 2013: 205)

Technologically deterministic discourses such as that put forward by Lee, position us a subject to technological imperatives which deny us any influence over the direction of technological development. In contrast, the SST family offers a theorisation whereby technology is not seen as neutral with its own inner logic, completely free from human intervention. Technology is seen as inherently political, contestable and has, in conjunction with us, the potential to travel along a variety of routes during its life. The SST approach has been shown to be useful in making sense a wide range of artefacts. Previous studies for instance have examined refrigerators, missile guidance systems, electric lighting, the bicycle, the telephone and videotext, radio, telephony, and electric media and computing and organisational technologies (see (MacKenzie and Wajcman 1985, Bijker 1987, Bijker et al. 1987, Bijker and Law 1994, Bijker 1995, Abbate 1999, Mackenzie and Wajcman 1999, Oudshoorn and Pinch 2005, Pinch 2005, Light and Wagner 2006, Boczkowski and Lievrouw 2008, Howcroft and Light 2010, Lauer 2012)). It has been suggested that historians and sociologists of technology have focused on technology as their major topic of analysis, whereas those who do cultural and media studies have primarily attended to users and consumers (Oudshoorn and Pinch 2005, Flanagin et al. 2010). My intention here is to attend to users and consumers and technology. However, I mean technology in the broadest sense, therefore alongside the typical "old" and "new media" that one might expect in a study such as this (such as telephones, televisions and forums), you will find mention of arrangements such as stairs, bus stops, vehicles and photocopiers as contributors to the appropriation of SNSs.

SST is not a single theory, like the phenomenon it is enrolled to shed light on, it is subject to ongoing work interspersed with moments of stability and includes a range of concepts and objects of study (Russell and Williams 2002, Flanagin et al. 2010). However, the SST family of theory is often discussed in terms of three main, frequently interwoven, themes – the social construction of technology (SCOT), the confusingly entitled social shaping of technology (SST) and actor–network theory (ANT). It is these three themes which I will now turn to.

Introducing SCOT, SST and ANT

SCOT draws from thinking related to the sociology of scientific knowledge (SSK) (Pinch and Bijker 1984, Bijker et al. 1987, Bijker et al. 1989, Russell and Williams 2002). SSK, a strand of the sociology of science, focuses on the processes by which the content of science, its theories and practices are brought into being. An underlying focus of SSK is to demonstrate the socially constructed nature of scientific knowledge in order to rebuff deterministic claims of neutrality. SCOT proponents apply the same logic to the analysis of technology and particularly technological development. SCOT stands as a response to technologically deterministic accounts of technological innovation, emphasising the importance of the social and the possibility for failure along the way. This focus on failure, in addition to successful outcomes, is rooted in the notion of symmetry. SCOT demands that there is symmetry in accounts of technological development. Therefore, for example in the case of this text, SNSs need to be understood in terms of their connective and disconnective possibilities. SCOT analyses incorporate attention to relevant social groups – those who compete to have their shared interests or problems taken care of during the innovation process. The differences in interpretations amongst these groups (which individuals may move between, co-exist in or leave), are understood via the concept of interpretive flexibility. Through this process, it is argued that closure is reached whereby the artefact in question comes into being. However, the potential for closure is contested. Closure does not imply a fixed state; there is always opportunity for arrangements to open up again and the process of negotiation regarding development to continue. Consequently, for some, stabilisation is referred to as this is said to imply a less fixed state of affairs (Bijker 1995). The assumptions associated with closure and stabilisation appear to be influenced by the nature of many SCOT (and indeed other more general SST) studies that have focused on less malleable arrangements such as Bakelite. Bakelite, or polyoxybenzylmethylenglycolanhydride, is a resin-based early form of hard plastic.

Here, it has been argued that one needs to bear in mind that the physical malleability of objects can affect how they can be designed and interpreted (Hutchby 2001). This is the case with Bakelite. Once formed into the shape of a door handle or light switch for instance, Bakelite affords few opportunities for interpretive flexibility or innofusion. Of course such engagements are possible – a door handle could, conceivably, be used as a weapon, it can also be seen as a product to be sold or as a way of making progress from one room to another in house. But, usually, once set, a door handle is most likely to remain a door handle. In contrast, where the digital is concerned, we are talking of arrangements that are, potentially, constantly malleable making attempts at reaching stabilisation or closure much more difficult to pronounce. For instance, in the case of this text, so many actors are involved in the constant co-production and consumption of SNSs, that completely determining what they are is potentially futile. The most we can hope for is some temporary shared understandings amongst a diversity of relevant social groups. Potential criticisms of SCOT are its heavy focus on the design stage of technologies, falling short of contexts of use (Winner 1999, Oudshoorn and Pinch 2005), and as many commentators have remarked, it said little about the social structure and power relationships within which technological development takes place (Mackay and Gillespie 1992). SCOT arguably attended very much to the socially constructed nature of technology and its development in its desire to leave behind technologically deterministic discourses. Such accounts left out the shaping effects that technology may have on sociality (Pinch and Bijker 1986, Russell 1986). This attention to the social influences on design often left out politics and macro/structural affects upon technological development. SST within the overall SST family takes up this position.

SSTs sought to demonstrate how technological arrangements become inscribed with social interests, especially those that might be seen as the dominant social interests in any given time. The 1985 SST reader by MacKenzie and Wajcman (1985) is a key text in this respect. This body of work, for example, included studies of the gendered nature and effects of technological arrangements, workplace technology design and military technology (MacKenzie and Wajcman 1985, Akrich 1992, Oudshoorn et al. 2004). SSTs informed work, focusing on the analysis of political, economic and cultural values, as related to sociotechnical arrangements asking questions of why some options are preferred over others. Winner (1999), for example, put forward two ways of understanding how artefacts have politics. His first conception refers to those artefacts that have politics written into them to help settle a particu-lar issue in society – an example here are spreadsheets used to allocate resources depending upon some pre-figured allocation arrangement. His second conception is those artefacts that are inherently political, as they appear to require, or to be strongly compatible with, particular kinds of political relationships. Nuclear weapons figure in this mode because, as Winner suggests, they demand a particular set of arrange-ments associated with their existence (such as armed forces). Whilst similarly concerned with questions of sociality, the lens deployed via SST researchers initially focused on macro issues, in comparison to SCOT researchers' early interest with the micro.

Early versions of SCOT and SST were concerned very much with what might be regarding as a socially deterministic take on technolog-ical development. A socially deterministic perspective on technological development is perhaps not surprising, and was arguably needed at the time, in order to challenge the technologically deterministic dis-courses that operated not just within society, but also the academy. Of course whilst technological determinism is still rife in certain parts of the academy and is very much woven into contemporary commer-cial and public policy, there are now many more who understanding things differently. However, alongside SCOT and SST, another body of work emerged – that of ANT (Latour 1987, Callon 1989, Law 1992, Latour 2005). ANT seeks to take seriously the non-human as an actor within sociotechnical arrangements, or actor–networks. However, ANT does not subscribe to technologically deterministic accounts of appro-priation. ANT brings to the fore the mutual shaping that is involved in our everyday interactions with technology. That deemed social and that deemed technical in such arrangements moreover are not seen as separate entities, instead they are conceptualised as coming into being where they interact. The coming into being of a set of arrangements involves a distinction between intermediaries and medi-ators. Intermediaries are argued to merely pass things along within the network while mediators engage in transformation work and are those that matter. Importantly mediators can be human or non-human and, from an ANT perspective, are argued to be equal. Such a treat-ment of non-human mediators is controversial with some arguing this is not possible since "things" cannot have intentionality or moral-ity. However, the point ANT advocates make is that agency does not necessarily go hand in hand with intentionality and morality – a door my close due to the wind and break someone's finger, for example.

Since its inception in the 1980s, SST theorists have moved towards a shared understanding of key issues within this body of work and there appears to be a greater willingness to combine different approaches. In sum, the family of theories, concepts and approaches that one might see as SSTs share a fundamental position that society has the potential to shape technology and that technology has the potential to shape society. This text has been written with an SST theorisation of appropriation in mind; however, I do not subscribe to one specific theory, concept or approach – rather I position my work in relation to this as way of making my philosophical, ontological and epistemological assumptions apparent up front. Drawing from SCOT, I am interested in how different social groups flexibly interpret different arrangements and how such arrangements become stabilised or not. I am also interested in meta-narratives regarding the sociotechnical and my analysis is influenced by the 1985 SST reader. I am also interested in acknowledging the role of the non-human in my analysis and therefore am influenced by ANT somewhat too. That said, I do not propose to scatter SST vocabulary liberally throughout the rest of this text. Instead I ask my readers to have such thinking in their in their minds as they read on. They might also notice this in my more general language and tone. I write of SNSs doing things *with* us for instance. In the next section I will further expand upon how an SST lens may help us view and think about processes of technological development.

Conceptualising technological development

Social shaping approaches attempt to illuminate the way that technologies are configured throughout appropriation *along with* various actors in different social groups (Bijker and Law 1994). Underlying this is a need to recognise the ongoing work that is required to make things operate beyond the design room. Technological development is therefore not seen as a linear process with one possible outcome, but rather as a process during which the form of an artefact becomes stabilised as consensus emerges among relevant social groups. Consequently, such accounts are not restricted to the social groups of design-room engineers, laboratory personnel and the like (Bijker 1994). However, the role of designers, of course, is not ruled out of our experiences of appropriation. Designers are argued to inscribe their visions of the future world into a given set of arrangements – for example, notions of how the technology should be used and in what contexts. In this respect Akrich (1992) enrols the metaphor of a film as such arrangements are characterised as putting forward a script which brings with it a preferred reading (the designer's reading) for the user. Of course, Akrich acknowledges these preferred readings may be adapted, edited or indeed rewritten. In a similar vein, Woolgar (1991) discussed designers' attempts to configure the user and how this might constrain appropriation though this position has been subject to critique as overemphasising the power of designers (Wajcman 1991, Berg and Lie 1995, Oudshoorn 1999, Mackay et al. 2000). In contrast, the downplaying of designers and the emphasis upon users is well articulated within the key work of Roger Silverstone regarding processes of domestication (Silverstone 1996, 2006). Domestication refers to the appropriation of objects by users in everyday life, and more specifically, the home (Silverstone and Hirsch 1992, Silverstone et al. 1992, Kline and Pinch 1996), although others have extended its application to other contexts (e.g. see the collection by Lie and Sørensen (1996)). Therefore, as I discuss in greater detail in the next section of this chapter, actors of varying kinds are key to SST accounts of technological development.

The involvement of a diverse range of actors brings suggests a conceptualisation of such arrangements as "configurable technologies" subject to "innofusion" – innovation at the local level (Fleck 1994). Yet, design-centred models persist and with them a preoccupation with prior technological design. These have, however, also been critiqued through the idea of the design fallacy – the presumption that the primary solution to meeting user needs is to build ever more extensive knowledge about the specific context and purposes of various users into technology design (Stewart and Williams 2005b). The design fallacy rests on a position that if we reject technologically deterministic thought on technological development, and that if we acknowledge the ongoing work required regarding sociotechnical assemblages once outside the design room, then it becomes problematic to assume that designers can fully anticipate requirements and use a priori. The design and use of technologies are therefore not linked in a linear and simple way. As Roharcher (2005: 11) states: "This is not only a consequence of a lack of interaction between designers and users, but also points to the fact that social practices of use or cultural meanings of artefacts cannot be fully anticipated in the design phase and are only developed during the implementation of technologies. What we generally observe is an iterative process of the co-construction of technologies by designers and various groups of users and other actors."

Importantly here, it is necessary to signal that these "other actors" may well include those that we might see as non-human in the ANT tradition. For my purposes, mediators such as physical surroundings and objects alongside material affects of interfaces and functions of SNSs are important considerations. In sum, a view from SSTs tells us that the appropriation of digital media, and in the case of this text, SNSs in particular, is a messy, complicated and indeterminate process. Disconnective practice, which involves human and non-human actors, I will argue, is a key ingredient here in the making of SNSs as configurable technologies.

Conceptualising users and non-users

Another point of relevance is the nuanced conceptualisation of use that is embedded within SSTs. Inherent within SSTs is the idea of symmetry and therefore, whilst one might emphasise action through the inclusion of concepts, such as relevant social groups, interpretive flexibility, stabilisation and closure, such conceptualisations demand an alternate reading in terms of what does not happen and who is not included. There is a need to attend to what have been termed "non-relevant social groups" (Silverstone et al. 1992, Oudshoorn and Pinch 2005). In the book *How Users Matter*, Sally Wyatt, overviews a reconceptualisation of the category of non-use that includes voluntary and the involuntary aspects. Her preliminary taxonomy identifies four different types of non-users: resisters (people who have never used the technology because they do not want to), rejectors (people who no longer use the technology, because they find it boring or expensive or because they have alternatives), the excluded (people who have never used the technology, because they cannot get access for a variety of reasons) and the expelled (people who have stopped using the technology involuntarily because of cost or loss of institutional access) (Wyatt et al. 2002, Wyatt 2005: 76). She also refers to the work of Miles and Thomas (1995) who also suggest that it is necessary to acknowledge partial use. Moreover, it is important to recognise the complications that can arise where people speak on behalf of users (Roharcher 2005). As has been articulated widely in design processes generally, and in relation to information technologies, there are a number of audiences who may be users, producers, intermediaries or one and the same at any given time. These audiences may include primary and secondary users (Friedman and Cornford 1989, Ferneley and Light 2006); bystanders[1] (Ferneley and Light 2008), consultants and managers (Howcroft and Light 2006, Howcroft and Light 2010), developers/designers of complementary products and others who may act as gatekeepers or proxies for ultimate potential users (Stewart and Williams 2005a, Wyatt 2005). This process of participation (and I would add, non-participation) in appropriation has been conceptualised as a technological drama, whereby technology is designed not only to perform a material function but similarly to express and coercively reinforce beliefs about the differential allocation of power, prestige and wealth in a society (Pfaffenberger 1992).

Consequently, SST requires not just a focus on binaries of use and non-use, we need to focus upon the exercise of power and nuances within and across these typical categories presented in the literature, especially when it comes to SNS research. Again, the concept of disconnective practice, I argue, has value here because it destabilises our focus on development and use as connection, and shifts our view to consider the potentials of power through disconnection.

A brief note on power

Admittedly, what I discuss here is a grossly simplified interpretation of a significant area of study, but I felt it necessary to lay our some basic tenets regarding how I am conceptualising power in relation to connectivity and disconnection. Here, I am indebted to the comprehensive and far reaching work of (Lukes 1974; 1977; 2005), which has shaped my thinking in this area.

Power in a general sense is understood in many ways, for instance, as a thing – such as a military power, a particular faculty of body or mind and fundamentally as the ability to do or act. However, in academic terms, we are generally more interested in power as a contested concept and this leads to questions about the relevance and importance of different forms of power exercise. Power is exercised all the time, and what is of interest is contestable, but ultimately, requires some kind of judgement call regarding what is deemed to be significant (which, of course, itself is an exercise of power). In this sense then, we are interested in notions of manipulation, authority, influence and coercion. Power exercise, more accurately, is concerned with the making of action, or not, had things been otherwise. Importantly, as I have just pointed to in the previous section, power can be attributed to both humans and non-humans. Working with power dynamics then are well-trodden arguments regarding the potentials of agency versus the influences of structure. Arguments regarding agency attribute freedom to undertake, and importantly not undertake, action to agents. The proposition is that of an existence of free will. In effect, it assumes that if I want to wear a skirt to work, I will. However, this of course assumes that when we exercise power, or not, we always have a choice in the matter. The logic of this position is that those who are subject to the exercise of power would have acted, thought and desired differently but for the exercise of power. This is where structure is enrolled.

Structures as enablers, parameters or constraints in a given context and can be seen as those things that set the limits of agency. Therefore, structure could be argued to be predominantly influential in the shaping of what we choose to do or not do. Here, I might not wear a skirt to work because I fear being harassed on my way to work on the bus. I might fear harassment if the social structures of contemporary Brisbane commuter travel do not sit well with a man being dressed in what are seen, by the majority of the population, as women's clothes. The structural constraints governing my choice here though, go beyond those I have constructed as concerned with contemporary Brisbane commuter travel. One has to think more broadly of the nature of structural constraints. There are many ways to do this, but Steven Lukes offers three. First, constraints can be external (where others/other things exclude you from options you might want) or internal (where you yourself do not even conceive of possibilities open to you for action). Second, structures can act positively by presenting obstacles that prevent you from taking the action you want to or they can act negatively where they do not provide the support for actions you want to take. Finally, structures can be used to limit the range of possibilities of action you have available to you or they can limit access to the means by which you might want to achieve certain actions. That said, structures are contested too. Indeed what is counted as a structure is relative to other matters, such as a given time or place. Therefore, it might be that if I catch the right bus I could happily wear a skirt as all the other skirt-wearing men of Brisbane are catching that one too. Therefore, what I am also pointing to here is a period of social transformation where structures may change and allow for agency. However, if we think of the world being characterised by structural determinism, then there would be no need for power as we would have to do what the structures "said". In effect, we could not have acted differently. Therefore we end up in a position whereby we have to recognise the potentials of agency and structure for shaping the exercise of power. In the light of such thinking, Lukes (1974) puts forward a three-dimensional view of power:

- 1DV: A has power over B because they can get B to do something they would not do otherwise. (It is made law that men cannot ride Brisbane public transport in skirts)

- 2DV: Power is exercised where the scope of decision-making is constrained and conflict suppressed. (Men can only wear skirts on Brisbane public transport if they are made of nylon)
- 3DV: Power is exercised by creating conditions so that conflict does not arise in the first place. (Men would never think of trying to board a bus in Brisbane, wearing a skirt, because they are conditioned to think this is not an option, and this is the case even though they might get some enjoyment from doing this if they tried it)

So what does this mean for SNSs and the position I take here? In short, what I hope emerges throughout the rest of the text is an analysis which demonstrates the complexity of the workings of agency and structure involving humans and non-humans where SNSs are concerned. This complexity is charged with different forms of power, as put forward by Lukes, and it is central to our navigations with connectivity and disconnectivity.

3
Acknowledging Mediators

Introduction

We know that non-human things affect our everyday lives and present us with continuities and discontinuities. In the UK, for example, the Teletext service, offered from the 1970s, gave viewers who purchased appropriately configured television sets the ability to use it as a daily reference source in the same way that they might use a newspaper. Video recorders further changed television by affording viewers greater control over the source and time of entertainment (Negrine and Goodfriend 1988). SNSs, such as Facebook and Twitter, present such continuities in our life – they can interact with us as newscaster and entertainment scheduler. Indeed, implicit interactivity was available pre-Web 2.0. The creators of hypertext technology envisioned it as challenging linearity and authorship (Jackson 1997). Interactivity (and implicitly the Internet as actor) was built into the Internet from the start (Abbate 1999, Flanagin et al. 2010). Ironically, Web 2.0-enabled SNSs, which are often pitched as highly interactive, also reintroduce regulated linearity via timelines and feeds. However, that is not to say that the early HTML-based hypertext-fuelled personal home pages of the early Web were not constraining. Arguably, it was not uncommon for individuals to take a cue from the architecture and tone of the online provider and condition their self-performances accordingly in such environments (Papacharissi 2002a, 2002b). In summary, the non-human has and continues to matter to us.

Digital media and specific communication applications and devices, such as email, instant messenger and mobile telephony, have, we are told, led to us into an age of perpetual contact. Here, an emphasis is placed on technologies being crucial drivers of connectivity. Indeed, even in more contemporary "Web 2.0" contexts (and as I alluded to in the previous chapter), nuanced accounts of technological change suggest a key role for digital technologies. As has been stated elsewhere, the "2.0" part of Web 2.0 lies in the collaborative and communicative elements, with the only significant technological change facilitating this being an increase in the bandwidth of home connections (Everitt and Mills 2009). Everitt and Mills are clearly critical of the pronouncements of technological determinists, and I agree with them that human elements are key. Nevertheless, I also think that there is more to talk about regarding the roles of technology beyond the increases in broadband Internet access. In this respect, one might then think, of course, that software code and algorithms matter too.

Talk of code and algorithms has become incredibly popular in academic discourses regarding the Internet, particularly over the past few years – especially in relation to the generation and analysis of the big data made by our engagements with SNSs. Such discussion and thought, however, is broader than this and has been in existence for longer. For example, several authors have pointed to the influence of code and/or algorithms in our lives (Feenberg 1992, 1995, Mitchell 1995, Adam 2005, Grimmelmann 2005, Lessig 2006, Introna 2007). Moreover, it has been argued that we interact with technologies that have "cognitive potential" (see Hayles in Gane et al. 2007). In this mode, we will only play a small part in interactions amongst non-human actors with much being hidden from view. It is this black boxing of technology, and the extent of its unknown/known influences, that seems to me, to be at the top of the agenda in contemporary discussions regarding code and algorithms and the role of the non-human where SNSs are concerned:

> The integration of networked technologies into everyday social practices compels us to reflect deeply on their protocols, platforms, and interface; the production of space is increasingly dependent on code, and code is written to produce space. Social media as a form of code is thus actively shaping sociospatial organisation, processes, and economies, along with discursive and material cultures.
>
> (Tierney 2013: 103)

In this chapter, I want to pay particular attention to the extent and nature of the engagements we have with things beyond the human in our everyday appropriation of SNSs – non-human mediators. However, unlike prior and on-going work, I intend, rather unfashionably, to step back from the intricacies of code and algorithms. I want to focus on less granular level digital mediators, and also, those that are not digital. I am interested in what comes from and encapsulates code and algorithms in a very broad sense. In particular, in support of my thesis regarding disconnective practice, I demonstrate how such mediators are implicated or not in a number of ways. To begin, I will briefly discuss contexts of appropriation in terms of geography, time and situated use – the where, the when and the with, if you like. I will then examine in more detail the work of applications, the functions they have, the interfaces they present themselves to us through, the devices we engage with them via and the infrastructures upon which they and we engage.

It is important to note here that I make no claim as to the accuracy of research participants' interpretations of their engagements. Participants may misrepresent the functions of various SNSs or may misunderstand them. This does not invalidate their view as for them they are identifying a benefit, problem, issue as they see it, and I am interested in this in terms of how it helps us understand the theoretical nature of SNSs appropriation. Moreover, a further complicating factor is the shifting nature of SNSs and the other mediators associated with them. What is present in a particular way at one point, might not be at another, due to the ongoing work being put into them, particularly by those who develop technology.

Where do mediators come from?

In the rest of this book I intend to go into significant detail regarding the contexts (and indeed content) of the appropriation of SNSs. However, here I wanted analyse this in terms of how contexts open the door for a variety of mediators to engage with us. The first way I want to think about this is as related to the idea of geography. The variety of experiences here are diverse, as experienced-user Katie enthusiastically proclaimed in relation to her sites of use: "Everywhere, on the toilet, in bed, in the bath, just everywhere constantly." But broad SNS use is not just for tech professionals, such as Katie, of course – diversity of appropriation space is vernacular:

> Well...I use it all over, you know...be sat on the couch, sometimes I'll have a quick look whilst I'm laid in bed. I generally tend not to use it on the toilet, which seems to be a general thing for people, sit on the toilet and just...I don't tend to do that. It's like a big germ receptacle when you're sat on the toilet. Er, that's about it really, you know I might sit in the garden, I've got coverage there. Even if the

Wi-Fi doesn't work, I've got normal coverage. I use it at work, not when I'm on the train but...when I've got frequent breaks I'll have a look.

(Matt, train driver, 35–44)

When talking with people it was clear that nowhere in the house was off limits. This opens up the range of mediators in those spaces that act to potentially shape the SNS experience. While Matt says above he wouldn't use it in the toilet because of germs, Kerry had a different take stating that "it's a moment of sitting down time, isn't it, which you don't get a lot". Kerry and Matt also talked about how vehicles mediated their SNS experience – Matt because he would not look at his phone whilst driving a train at work, Kerry because reading in a car made her feel ill. Moreover, it was also clear that use was equally diverse whether this was in a personal context as discussed particularly in the next chapter or at work as discussed in Chapter 5. My point here is that it is not just the materiality of code and algorithms at play here – other objects enter our SNS space and influence our engagements whether these be toilets, vehicles, beds, sofas, kitchen tables and, as we shall see in later chapters, cafés, public seating arrangements, photocopiers and takeaway counters.

The points in time that SNSs are engaged with are equally diverse, bringing with them another lens for identifying non-human mediators:

On the couch generally, occasionally in bed I suppose, not very often just very briefly, just seconds sometimes. Well actually, I got into a habit, I don't know if it's good or bad, but if I wake up in the morning I'm usually in a complete fog, I don't even know what day it is, and it helps, if I want to wake up and just be awake, then I can read my Twitter feed or whatever. It just takes 2 minutes to read the latest stuff and that's just alerted me enough, made my eyes wake up and made me concentrate enough to know what day it is and then get out of bed. I don't know whether it is a good idea but I do do it.

(Kevin, sales assistant, 25–34)

Most of the people I interviewed mentioned waking up and going to bed with SNSs, whether this was checking status updates and messages or using services, such as Spotify or YouTube, to play music through them. This specific context of use led to discussions about the particular arrangement of objects, such as pillows, tables and electrical sockets in order to create an appropriate set up. Where Lessig states "code is law" it would seem that for many, so are home furnishings. Indeed, very similar arrangement codes could be identified throughout peoples' homes, as they were on the move in public space and at work.

However, although I want to remind the reader of the importance of other arrangements beyond the digital, it is important not to forget such mediators. As part of the assemblages of use discussed by my participants, was the phenomenon of mixed use which has particularly been brought out in studies of young people's appropriation of the Internet and especially as concerned with conceptulisations of the so called digital native. In my work, I also saw it amongst other age groups. A particular feature was the use of SNSs whilst watching television. As Denise said: "Some nights I'm very active on Twitter, say if it's a big news event or a big TV talking point." Yet, it has recently been argued that many still consider the Internet as separate from television; as something that exists in a different realm, engaged within a different room, and conceived of and produced in a separate production sphere (Young 2011). Young continues to argue that this approach tends to conflate the Internet with the amateur and ignores the technically convergent shift towards Internet distribution by large sections of the media industries (e.g. television via Hulu, iView, iPlayer, iTunes and YouTube). What Denise's experience also reminds us is that the Internet, and particularly SNSs, have moved into the living room and are being engaged with at the same time as television is used whether this is to tweet alongside programming or as a something to do in addition to keeping an eye on what is happening on the television screen.

Such mixed media use assemblages also arose out of a perceived necessity rather than just a desire to engage with multiple media. For example, Sarah stated:

> If I'm on two different things on the same site, say on Facebook, I'm on a chat on the computer then I'm doing other stuff on the phone so I can check my messages and be on chat at the same time and stuff like that. I probably could [do it all via one interface on the my computer] but it's harder, you have to have loads of windows open, my way is easier.
>
> (Sarah, call centre worker, 16–24)

Others mentioned additional media use because of work constraints. Aleksy said that he had to access SNSs via his phone whilst also using his work PC because SNS sites were blocked at work. Kevin on the other hand, purposefully connected three devices (his phone, iPad and PC) so that they shared information amongst each other, to create what he called "a circuit, a network in itself". Context therefore invites a broad range of mediators into our SNS practices.

Applications

I want to examine some of the ways in which different SNS applications, such as Facebook and Twitter, present the opportunity to mediate our activity or not. By application, I mean that software which enables a computing device to engage a user in some kind of activity. Therefore, I am interested in applications that run in browsers on PCs and those that are downloadable "apps" for mobiles and tablets and increasingly PCs. Of course SNSs can also be conceptualised as platforms. Here, I am not interested SNSs as development environments as this takes me into the realm of code and algorithms which is outside the parameters of this particular piece of work.

We know that the distinctiveness of online identity expressions can be attributed to the purposes and structural features of particular online spaces, as well as the people who frequent them (Davis 2012). As Baym (2010) states, different sites influence self-presentation in different ways, such as by providing visible links to other people or offering attire and accoutrements to build identities. Indeed, some SNSs have been argued to be more attuned to identity work than others. For example, it has been argued that that the architecture of MySpace provides a format for actors to overtly disclose who they are, or who they want to present themselves as (Davis 2010). In contrast it has been argued that Facebook's social newsfeed is now at the core of its functionality which demotes autobiographical detail, including lists of favourite bands, books and television shows (Robards 2012).

Such architectural differences also attempt to shape the overall nature of interactions and relationships within a particular space. For example, Twitter has been put forward as having a "directed friendship" model where participants choose Twitter accounts to "follow" and they each have their own group of followers. However, there is no technical requirement of reciprocity, and often, no social expectation of it either (Marwick and boyd 2011b). Further, via a comparative analysis of the Facebook, LinkedIn and ASmallWorld, Papacharissi (2009) highlights the private/public balance present in each SNS; their respective styles of self-presentation in spaces privately public and publicly private; the cultivation of taste performances; and the formation of tight or loose social settings. Papacharissi further unpacks the latter point characterising Facebook via the metaphor of a glasshouse with a publicly open structure, looser behavioural norms. LinkedIn and ASmallWorld are presented as tighter spaces. Such behavioural norms can be experienced in a number of ways. For example, Matt said:

> I don't lie, I find Facebook a lot more superficial and trivial and I find most people probably wouldn't be interest in some of the stuff I read on there, whereas Twitter's got a different sort of user base for me. They're two separate circles really. But a lot of crossover with friends and things like that, but generally there's a lot of people on Facebook that probably wouldn't even understand words [laughs]. Sorry.
>
> (Matt, train driver, 35–44)

Whilst Kerry takes a different view:

> So, I always fancied getting into Twitter but I just don't understand it; I just can't grasp it. I don't know what all these hashes mean, or @such and such. I don't get it. I want to learn it but I've never had the time to sit down with it. . . . It's like a secret code that I feel I need to crack. But I don't really know it very well. So I stick to Facebook because I know what I'm doing.
>
> (Kerry, local government worker, 35–44)

Overall though, Papacharissi makes important points here about the overall nature of and philosophy underlying different SNSs. Such philosophy was perhaps most clearly articulated in relation to Facebook, for example, by Mark Zuckerberg who in January 2010, told the audience at the Crunchie awards held in San Francisco, that: "People have really gotten comfortable not only sharing more information and different kinds, but more openly and with more people. That social norm is just something that has evolved over time" (Johnson 2010). Arguably, this was in fact more a statement about his vision for Facebook and the changes the company were making to the features of its application than it was a genuinely engineered shift in social attitudes. But further, later characterisations of Facebook as, for example that "Facebook Doesn't Want To Be Cool, It Wants To Be Electricity" (Constine and Ferenstein 2013), point to other philosophical positions beyond those related to publicness and privacy. Such pronouncements, which conceive of Facebook as a utility, point to the desire for it to be indispensable and central to people's lives; in this case, their lives with the Internet in much the same way as Goggin (2009) points to the shaping of the iPhone as a device to navigate, arrange and orchestrate everyday life. In this mode, Facebook is not just a glasshouse, it is the house that everyone goes to; it positions itself as wanting to be the Internet. This desire translates then into a "pull" mentality regarding the site – Facebook is something that you bring things into, not push things out from. YouTube, for example almost operates in reverse by allowing people the ability to distribute content widely with other applications, such as Twitter and, of course, Facebook. Twitter, one might argue strikes a balance between the two – drawing people and content in by allowing people to build communities with the application and follow key people, such as celebrities, as well as allowing content to be distributed widely via SNSs and other social media.

Smartphone apps

Smartphone apps, or as Daphne called them, "the little logo on the phone" are a popular way of mediating access to SNSs and were perceived to have benefits. Kevin, for instance, talked of how he liked the fact that apps filled his screen and were easy to scroll through: "it's just neater and it just works nicer". However, many participants were frustrated by apps in a number of ways. Some were aware of functionality being absent from an app as compared to the browser-based version of the SNS site. For example, Nina reported being unable to change her cover photo on Facebook, Jenny told of how she was unable to direct her photos to a specific folder if she uploaded to Facebook via the smartphone app and Simon spoke of not being able to use the same Facebook app for multiple identity management (he has two accounts – one for him and one for his alter ego). Sarah also found the app to be annoying in that she perceived it as slow and did not like that fact that it constantly tried to get her attention by sending her notifications saying that they "do my head in".

Sarah's experience sits with another set where people talked of apps making it difficult for them to disconnect in a variety of ways. Where Sarah wanted not to be in contact with Facebook all the time, Ian wanted to be able to delete content he had maybe posted in haste, Rebecca and Aleksy wanted to be able to edit content they had uploaded. Nina further noted that she was unable to adjust her privacy settings for Twitter via her smartphone app. All these examples point to how apps colour people's experience of SNS appropriation whether this is to enable connectivity or to engage in disconnective practice.

Application functions

In terms of functions more generally as being within applications, one way of thinking about this is to distinguish between those functions that are performed manually and those which involve automation. In terms of manual functions, participants spoke of taking approaches to disconnecting with and within SNSs through the use of back channels:

> a friend of mine in another country messaged me one day to say "oh check this out", and 1 of these guys were obviously having an affair and had done what I'd done [accidentally, and publicly, make an explicit sexual comment to her partner] but to the person he was having an affair with, to the main Twitter timeline. And then 2 other academics in the U.S. had screen grabbed and then they posted it, they were really gossipy. So I make a lot of use of the Twitter back channel and I have quite a giggle about the fact that, and I'm quite open about it, I would be chatting to someone on Twitter and then I'll go "come on, back channel". I think the Twitter presence on the public timeline is very controlled and there's a point where you go "right I'm not going to say this publicly any more, let's direct message", and I think everyone uses it in that way.
>
> (Katie, social technologist, 35–44)

Here not only does Katie engage in back channel banter, she is quite open about that fact that she does this – she is telling others that she is disconnecting from the public Twitter feed to go and socialise elsewhere at the same time. It is also interesting to note that Katie assumes that because she uses Twitter in this way, everyone else does. I have found this to be a common take on SNSs – users often think everyone else does what they do with an SNS. In the same way as designers have been argued to set a vision for how a set of arrangements might be engaged with, so do users. But also back channels displayed further requirements for people to develop strategies to allow for disconnection. For example, as Andy explained:

> On the messages, on Facebook, they've now introduced it where you can see when the person has accessed the message and read it, and I think that's taking it a bit too far really, that's a bit too intrusive. Because before they didn't know and you could say "Ooh I've not seen it, I've not been on for a few days", but now you click on it

and they're like "well you saw it at 16:29, you've not responded yet". I just don't click on the messages now. One guy I was seeing about 13 years ago, and he was messaging me and trying to be a bit pally and stuff and get back in touch with me, and this was one thing that annoyed me as well, I didn't know how he knew that I kept logging on. And every time I logged on, I'd get a message from him, and I was thinking "how does Facebook know when you're logging on", but they introduced it whereby when you log on, it automatically logs you into chat and then people know you're online. And again, I think that's something a bit intrusive really because you might not, it's not that you're being nasty or that you don't want to talk to someone, you might be busy. But I didn't like that and I kept getting messages saying "oh hi Andy, how's it going, what's up, do you fancy meeting up". But then I realised that by turning that off, he didn't know, but still he knows when you've read his message, and I find that really intrusive.

(Andy, legal professional, 25–34)

Another manual disconnective practice with functions was exemplified by participants in terms of how they engaged with the sharing of posts within and particularly between sites. During the discussion about sharing practices in the interviews, it became clear that participants did not necessarily want this automated, or indeed they did not realise it could be. Hannah, for instance, talked of how she might find a video to share with people on Facebook on YouTube, but instead of clicking the share button she would simply cut and paste the URL from one site and into the relevant point in the target site. I call this *cut and paste connectivity*. Hannah particularly explained that she did not readily want to create information to profile her. Importantly, YouTube is complicit in cut and paste connectivity because it allows people to take the URL without being logged into a YouTube account and by offering this as an option in addition to share buttons.

The tensions between sharing and withholding information was a common thread of discussions in relation to engagements with automated functions too and is nicely articulated in Katie's story about Tripit (Table 3.1). However people did engage with automated functions. Jenny, for instance, used her Twitter log in details with for an app called Pocket which she described as creating reading lists for later. Sound as a function was also mentioned as playing a part – Xui Li recalled "whenever I get a notification I get the noise, so I check it instantly". Nina in particular liked the aesthetic quality of automated posting of URLs

Table 3.1 TripIt trips up Katie

TripIt the travel planner is another account I use, and TripIt has been a godsend to me because I do a lot of travelling and what it does, basically as your booking confirmations come into your email account, it just scans them and it builds your itinerary for you and so it just saves loads of time. I've got the app in my phone so if I'm travelling I can just go to the TripIt app and it tells me everything, my flight number, my hotel, stuff that I used to have to sit down and do manually, so it's absolutely brilliant. Because I have been away a lot, I've then started to feed TripIt, basically TripIt would notify LinkedIn and my professional Facebook when I was going to be away so people would know that I was away and stuff, which was really valuable. And then me and my partner split up in February, and months ago we had booked a holiday to Granada in Spain a couple of weeks ago, and all of a sudden a couple of weeks ago I had people writing on my Facebook wall "oh I hope you're having a great time, have a brilliant holiday", and people tweeting me, and I was like "what?". And then I realised that TripIt doesn't know that my relationship has ended and it was carrying on feeding out this holiday booking saying I'm just about to got to Granada for 5 days, so that was a bit of a weird one actually. Yes, and I've been on it in the past with regards to keeping on top of what platforms are talking to each other, but it's things like that. I've never ever filled in a Facebook relationship status in my life, I've always been quiet, just because I've seen it go to shit so many times with people, and then all of a sudden I got tripped up by TripIt basically telling everyone where I was at. So that was an interesting one, so then I had to explain to people "no I'm not going away, it was with blah blah, we have split up".

Katie, social technologist, 35–44.

with Twitter because it "doesn't look messy". Nina also saw value in automated functions in terms of connecting sites for building audiences across applications – but this was a temporary situation. Nina explained that initially she connected her Facebook, Tumblr and Twitter accounts in order to build up an audience on Twitter and Tumblr – the idea being that Facebook, where most of her connections where, would provide a boost to this audience. Once this had reached an acceptable level for her, she then disconnected the sites again.

Not only does Nina's activity demonstrate disconnective practice, it shows how users might seek to challenge the philosophy of a site and make it work for their own ends. Facebook, as Kevin said, "is like a Mall, it wants to keep you at the mall"; Nina went to the mall, met some friends and took them shopping elsewhere. Moreover, we also see that sites such as Tumblr and Twitter are actors here too in sense of them offering functions that offer the possibility of users discovering spaces beyond the walls of Facebook. Of course, not all sites afford this facility as Papacharissi states of ASmallWorld – it communicates verbally and spatially through an index page that is impossible to get past unless one possesses membership, exclusivity and the presence of a space that is truly private (Papacharissi 2009). I have observed a similar set of arrangements within Facebook via the use of closed and unpublicised groups, particularly for T-Girls/Transvestite members – an exclusive backchannel is created.

However, automated functions were also viewed sceptically. As will be shown through this text, there are parallel stories of varying attempts at resistance to connective functions. Such disconnective practices included turning off automated location-based data check-ins for sites such as Four Square, not using the same SNSs login details to access multiple services and not allowing applications to access content such as photographs on mobile devices as the following quotes demonstrate:

> I have so many to remember but I like having different passwords. So, you know, if someone gets hold of one password and they can't log into all of them.
>
> (Bob, cleaner, 25–34)

> ...it goes back to the logging into things with your Facebook account. Harvesting information, you know, they've sort of instigated "tag where you are", you know when you don't update "where are you, who are you with, where are you shopping". Foursquare does that doesn't it, have to check in everywhere and all these things, you know, I just find it a bit "Big Brother" which is probably the term you hear a lot of when people are talking about the internet. It's a bit Orwellian, isn't it?
>
> (Matt, train driver, 35–44)

> ...you're in something and it tries to take you through Facebook and I tend not to link those. I just don't like the thought of the linkage being too easy. I'm always careful. Well, there are bits of your life that have got money in them and you know what I mean.
>
> (Daphne, local councillor, 65+)

Others found such functions irritating. Sarah stated that she used to connect Facebook and Twitter, but stopped because it became annoying and Rebecca found that gaming apps within Facebook were posting on her behalf to friends and she didn't like that. Some participants found automated functions obstructive and the cause disconnection.

Interfaces

One of the tropes of Web 2.0, social media and SNSs has been that of increased ease of access in interface (and functional) terms as compared with prior versions of the Web. Yet is has been argued that the (now increasingly unfashionable) "glass shadow" graphics and cute icons that arrived with the 2.0 style had nothing to do with functionality, and more to do with creating as much distance as possible from so called geeks who may have been using similar technology for many years before (Everitt and Mills 2009). Interfaces then are not just visual guides, they are political as has been shown for instance in relation to race (Kolko 2000, Nakamura 2002) and gender and sexuality (Light 2007). So my first point is that SNSs interfaces do politics with us. For example, it has been noted that profile pages can be constricting in SNSs (Light 2007, Davis 2010, Cassidy 2013). Indeed Burgess (2014) goes further suggesting that the taglines so often a key feature of SNSs are not only representations of what they are "for", they are also performative. She argues that in the case of Facebook's "what's on your mind" or Twitter's "what's happening", they appear in close proximity to the user input boxes and therefore invite participation, at the same time suggesting what the normative purpose and nature of that participation is. However, the extent of the power of such taglines requires further investigation. Arguably the forms of updates provided by users are not always shaped by the tagline of the developer. Users learn "the rules" of updates not only from taglines, but also from others and their experiences of SNSs over time. SNSs are not just social but socialising and sometimes such socialisation can become so embedded, it is difficult for social practice to be changed merely by textual guidance from the developer regarding what to type in the box. Interfaces, as well as acting, can recede into the background and become taken for granted.

That said, the interface aesthetics can also influence disconnective practice as Katie suggests: "on the occasion I've looked at it on my phone I've just gone urgh I don't like that". The look of Facebook is one of the reasons Katie cited as to why she did not engage with Facebook very much. For others, they would not necessarily cease Facebook use because of its interface but they might only use it on particular devices:

> I do have the Facebook app on my iPad but I don't like it, I prefer to just log straight online... Because I guess you get used to a certain layout and it's not the same as the normal one is, and everything looks really big like its set out for a baby...
>
> (Hannah, sales assistant, 25–34)

Participants also discussed the more general problems they experience navigating and shaping interfaces. For example, Matt said of Facebook that he felt it was "near impossible to make sense of how to do your settings how you like them all.. you have to go through 15 screens and you don't find what you're looking for and ... meh" and Ian told of how he wanted to be able to adjust things but could not "there's a bit at the top of my page that asks for your name and your job, where you're living and all that. I just want to get rid of it but I can't, I don't know how to". However, it was not just the navigation and shaping of interfaces at a particular point in time that was at issue, participants also talked about the apparent constant change to SNSs, or as Everitt and Mills (2009) would term it, of being in perpetual beta. Indeed, as Suzanne recalled: "I'm upgrading things and I don't even know if I want it, but I don't want it really, just tells you it's there and I think ooh I should have it, but I don't need it."

Many participants reported difficulty adjusting to new interfaces they were presented with, often cited a preference for the previous iteration and could not understand why it had to be changed in the first place as they felt it was working okay. This feeling of it working okay is interesting given that all participants reported some kind of issue with the SNSs that they used suggesting that some of the interface/functional issues that they were raising, whilst problems, were forgotten in this context. However, some think that the changes might be attempts at improving the user experience, though they were unsure as to how these had been arrived at and the extent to which they would have any say, even when feedback was requested from the site's developers:

> I don't know whether they go through testing and they only broadcast it to a small number of people and see how they've found it, or whether it's just been a case of "right, this is the new version of Facebook, this is what you're stuck with" because I know when YouTube changed, how that was all done, it said you can

leave feedback which I did after a week of using it and they haven't changed it back. But all I can think of is well has anybody else said this so I've offered my opinion but am I the only one that thinks like this?

(Simon, civil servant, 25–34)

A further area of discussion was, of course, how the interface and associated functions might be changed as related to user privacy:

I remember about two years ago on Facebook they revamped their site without really warning or telling anyone. As part of that everyone's privacy settings were changed to basically become a free-for-all, so it meant that any photos you ever posted could be accessed and viewed by anybody that happened to find you on Facebook. I wasn't aware of this initially, and I didn't want kids seeing photographs of me, smoking and drinking at parties or whatever.

(Ian, school teacher, 35–44)

This is something I have also found in my ethnographic work on Facebook conducted with Kathy McGrath (Light and McGrath 2010). Through our disclosive analysis of Facebook we noted the constant change in interfaces. Figure 3.1 focuses upon the shifting nature of privacy within Facebook over time and I have updated it to include how privacy is presented to the user as of February 2014. As we noted in our original work,

...following the launch of a revised site in August 2008, the link named "privacy" on the user's Welcome page was demoted to a menu that only appeared when you held a mouse over it...This menu was labelled "Settings" and appeared with a padlock logo next to it. In February 2010, the site was again revised in this area. The menu was labelled "Account" and "Privacy settings" became one of seven options to choose from on a drop down menu. The padlock logo (arguably a sign synonymous with security) was also removed. What we see is the ability to mediate privacy becoming more distant. By way of contextualising this point, we note that the images shown in Figure 2 represent a very small area of the overall interface, which further obscures the path to mediating a user's profile.

(Light and McGrath 2010: 302)

What we see, in the revised version, is the return of the padlock, but it is much smaller than before. Privacy continues to recede into the

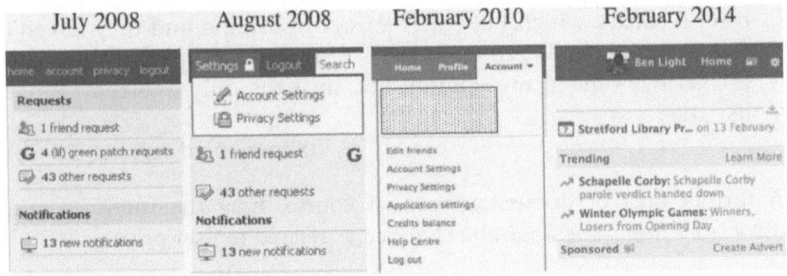

Figure 3.1   Changing interfaces of Facebook

background and one has to question Zuckerberg's assertion that our attitudes to this are something that have "just evolved over time" (Figure 3.1).

Devices

The devices that people engage with to access SNSs also figured in processes of appropriation. Such roles can be as related to the kinds of activity being performed and their context of enactment:

> If I was on Twitter on my laptop, I probably wouldn't be uploading pictures, whereas I suppose using it on my phone, that's probably where I would have taken the pictures on my phone and I would've uploaded them straight to Twitter from my phone. And as well, they have games on Facebook and I would say that I played them on my phone but not my computer.
>
> (Nina, sales assistant, 16–24)

Taking a different view, Ela said she would tend to use her phone to make comments in Japanese because she found it easier to do it on that somehow. This latter idea of ease was a broader consideration for others. This manifested itself in terms of how easy the device was to make operational. For example, Kerry said of her phone: "It's just easier, quicker. You can just click on your app and in a second you're in ... rather than sit down at the PC, switch it on ...", whereas Hannah preferred to use her laptop:

> I have to say using an iPad for Facebook, obviously you have to touch everything with your finger, it's a bit unresponsive sometimes and

my iPad's not even old so I don't think it's my iPad, I think it's just the whole iPad Facebook touching thing, it isn't so responsive. Yes, probably out of the two I probably would, ideally, use the laptop to go on Facebook because there's just a quicker response.

(Hannah, sales assistant, 25–34)

Additionally, Matt preferred accessing Twitter on his phone because he liked to stay logged on and felt safe doing so using that particular device – because only he used it and it had an access code only he know. In contrast, he said he could not stay logged into the laptop as other people had access to that. Therefore, the extent to which a device was accessible to Matt and to others had an influence upon patterns of appropriation. For some, the idea of personal access was also tied to the idea of always being able to access a device. Ian reported that 90% of his access was through his phone because he always carried it with him. He would only switch to another device if he wanted to "do something bigger", such as upload an album of photographs. This was also a way devices were implicated for Jenny who felt it was easier to deal with photo uploads if she used her computer.

A common point of discussion in the interviews in respect the role of devices, was the presence, or not, of a physical keyboard. Overall, people reserved input intensive tasks, such as writing long messages, for physical keyboards wherever possible, but were happy to use touchscreens for short messages, uploading small amounts of content and browsing:

I want to speak to my sister and I know it's going to be a longer conversation, I would probably use the laptop, that's handy. So it would depend on the length of the action.

(Aleksy, IT analyst, 25–34)

On my phone it would just be having a look, more of a passive consumption I would say. And then when I'm on the computer, that's when I would maybe upload photographs or actually send messages to people, just because it's a lot easier to use it like that.

(Jenny, school teacher, 25–34)

Device screens were also mentioned as mediators in a number of ways. Ela who had problems with her sight said that larger screens helped in this respect and Nina just thought her iPad screen was just "a bit nicer" than her laptop one. It was also noted that the reduced screen size of phones had implications for the design of the apps they ran:

> Oh yeah, it's scaled down for your phone because there is only so much information a phone can process. But the laptop, you get the full page, but it gets squished and squashed into your phone, and it's tiny. You can't do half of what you can do on the laptop, so it's very basic Facebook. But sometimes it's easier like that, actually, because there's no flashing adverts.
>
> (Bob, cleaner, 25–34)

Moreover, as Bob points out, people also were aware of the role of the processing power of the device in mediating access, especially on phones. This was something that Jason in particular noted saying that in the past he had used "low tech phones" that were ridiculously slow. Jason also mentioned how the storage capacity of his phone mediated his SNS use – he didn't like to fill it with photos, as he wanted that space for music instead. Sarah also mentioned the issue of space as a reason for not using SNS apps, stating they were too big and preferred to use them via her phone's browser instead.

Infrastructure

Infrastructure as mediator is also present in SNS appropriation. At the macro level, drawing on Lovnik (2011), this can involve the isolation of Internet protocol (IP) ranges, the addresses given to any given country, in an attempt to stop citizens of a given country from accessing SNSs. To date this has included countries such as China, Morocco and Thailand and even specific content with SNSs as in the case of music videos on YouTube in Germany. However, beyond this, at the micro level, users experience infrastructure as a mediator in a number of ways. For example, some participants talked of data allowances on mobile networks as being a consideration. As Ela stated "you have an option to just pick all the photos and it will upload it for you, but you have to pay for it, so you're using you're network allowance in terms of data". Of course, this is not a new phenomena, Livia (2002) discussed a similar concern with cost and data in respect of gay men's networking practices with the French Minitel system in the 1990s, where she noted that due to the high per-minute connection charges, users packed pseudonyms with a large amount of personal information so that time could be better spent on dialogue. Similarly, Gye (2007) noted how early multimedia messaging services (MMSs) were costly and consequently affected mobile phone photo-sharing practices as has been the expense of sending mobile phone created video clips (Chesher 2007).

The connection speed of infrastructure was also mentioned as being relevant. This related to Wi-Fi networks, where, for example, Julie said she experienced problems with her connection if she moved her laptop downstairs, so she had to access SNSs upstairs in her study. Also, Xui Li reported that her Wi-Fi connection at home could be unstable:

> I live in a flat on the top floor, three flights of stairs and I really don't want to go down and back up them all. Sometimes someone sends me a message but before you even look at it the Internet's gone down, so then I think "Oh, phone it is!"
>
> (Xui Li, student, 16–24)

Xui's experience illustrates how if one piece of infrastructure is absent another might be enrolled. The use of mobile phone networks as a surrogate for Wi-Fi networks was also mentioned by other participants. Similar to Xui, Simon reported getting a better connection at home with his phone rather than with his Wi-Fi, whereas Jason used it as an additional connection when his Wi-Fi was being fully utilised for downloads:

> ...because I download a lot of stuff, the actual connection on the computer slows down considerably once I've got things downloading. So if I want to contact someone through Facebook, when my computer is downloading stuff, I might then go onto the app on my phone because I never have a problem with the connection that way.
>
> (Jason, unemployed/charity volunteer, 25–34)

However, for some, such as Jenny and Daphne, they found that 3G signals could be weak and slow in some contexts and they would not connect to SNSs until they could access Wi-Fi either at home or on the move somewhere else. A final infrastructural consideration that was put forward was access to power. Nina talked of how she would limit YouTube use whilst travelling on the train as it drained the battery in her phone. Infrastructure therefore matters in terms of our abilities to connect, and also disconnect.

Conclusion

In this chapter, I have attempted to shed light on the range of mediators that might be implicated in our engagements with SNSs. My focus
has mostly been on digital mediators of some kind; however, as I have
pointed out, it is important to acknowledge others. As a reminder, a few
examples of non-digital mediators mentioned by participants included
the germs associated with toilets, bodies as experienced with vehicles
and vehicles as intimately tied with legal structures. As part of my interrogation of the context made up with mediators, I also noted the role
of mixed use of media devices and the potentials for our own attention
capabilities to lead us into momentary disconnective practices. Indeed,
as I complete this book, several media stories have surfaced lament-
ing the loss of living in the moment as we purportedly scramble to
document our lives. Yet, although we can be disconnected from our
surroundings whilst engaged with digital media, I do not see this as
much different from a range of preceding assemblages – being the driver
through areas of outstanding natural beauty or reading a book on a
train. For me, there is a snobbery associated with such discourses – as
my partner and I often say to each other, with a laugh, we can do both!

Within the context of appropriation of SNSs, key mediators are the
applications themselves. I refer to the applications we might use via
Web browsers and those we access via a dedicated piece of software on a
tablet, smartphone or other device. Also, the inscribed philosophies of
SNSs can affect connectivity in particular ways and, importantly, engage
with us in disconnective practice. The need for an account to access a
site and the extent to which data can be shared between one site and
another are examples of how disconnective practice may be brought
into existence, or not. The features and functions of applications/apps
are perhaps the most obvious actors to allow for the engagement of
disconnective practice, whether these are manually sourced, such as
the use of cut and paste connectivity, or more automated in nature via
the cessation of location-sharing features. I have also pointed to how the
interfaces of applications can lead to disconnective practices, whether
this is due to ugly presentation, complexity or something else.

Going beyond the application, the devices upon which sites are
accessed can engage with users in disconnective practice. For the people in the study, this involved considerations related to loading times,
screen size, storage capacity and the presence of, or not, of a physical
keyboard. The infrastructure with which SNSs operate was also mentioned as a mediator of practice. Beyond the blocking of IP ranges

in terms of content and country, mobile data allowances, connection speeds, connection strengths and access to electricity/battery power were all mentioned here.

Throughout the rest of this text, I tend to emphasise human agency much more than the non-human as this was the route the interview data took me. The humans in this case presented more as mediators though I do not doubt that other studies could indicate otherwise. In any event, I hope this chapter acts as a helpful sensitizer to the value of considering the role of non-human mediators in relation to SNS appropriation. Moreover, I think it clearly demonstrates how non-human mediators are implicated with us in disconnective practice.

Part II
Public Disconnection

Part II
Public Disconnection

4
Shaping Publics

Introduction

Mobility in various forms has been argued to be a feature of modern life, in different ways for many years, whether it is the mobility of ourselves (Sennett 1978), or how it is talked about as enabled by various forms of mobile and ubiquitous computing (Weiser 1991, Weiser and Brown 1997, Weiser et al. 1999, Russell et al. 2005). Such developments have been argued to transgress the boundaries of social situations (Waskul and Douglas 1997) and have changed the relationships between the public and the private, and the online and the physical (Kakihara et al. 2002, Middleton and Cukier 2006). Public spaces are now those where we can work and hang out with digital media (Hampton and Gupta 2008). SNSs have been incorporated into these arrangements and have been shown to hold the potential to change the way we experience public space (Humphreys 2007). In this chapter, I will explore how we might participate with SNSs in the mediation of public life, and more specifically public life that goes beyond the boundaries of work and home – for example, in cafés, as we shop and as we commute. Related to this, I want to consider SNSs in terms of how they and we are implicated in the construction of further public spaces and the extent to which these reflect more general interpretations of decent behaviour. I am interested here, given the technologically deterministic discourses of perpetual contact we are presented with in the mass media, in how disconnective practice is implicated. How is disconnective practice implicated in our navigation of public spaces with and within SNSs both in terms of what we do and what we are allowed to do? We know this is occurring from prior research into SNSs that argues we constantly make these things work for us as best we can. We also know such navigation is occurring as those who study mobile and ubiquitous computing highlight the potentials of our engagements with these to allow for us to be close and distant, private and public, busy and available (Arnold 2003).

However, it is perhaps helpful here for me to briefly set out what I mean by public for my purposes. At their very simplest, I see publics as spaces in which we do things alongside others, in an open fashion, and where there is not an expectation of complete privacy. I emphasise not an expectation of complete privacy, as public and private are not a mutually exclusive binary. Private spaces are possible within public space; consider telephone booths, public toilets and the use of personal audio devices. Publics of course have many purposes and uses and have been theorised accordingly. For instance, publics can be seen as: incorporating common understandings of a given space (Livingstone 2005); deliberative spaces (Habermas 1991); and as sites of domination, exclusion and regulation which produce subaltern counter publics (Fraser 1990). More specifically, where digital media are concerned, public space has been discussed in a number of ways. Here I want to particularly focus upon the notion of networked publics. In this respect, there is some research that pre-dates SNSs. Johnson's (1997) work, in particular, articulated a framework for what she termed, understanding the characteristics of communications in computer-based networks. This framework incorporated ideas of:

- scope – electronic networks can offer greater reach over physical networks;
- anonymity – individuals can communicate via the use of pseudonyms and personas; and
- reproducibility – information can be reproduced online without a loss of value – it can be recorded, observed and persistent.

One might see Johnson's work as a way of articulating a form of networked public prior to the emergence of SNSs as we know them today. Post the emergence of SNSs, Ito introduced the term networked publics to reference a linked set of social, cultural and technological developments that have accompanied the growing engagement with digitally networked media. Here the idea is used to focus on how people respond to and are (re)makers of media (Ito 2007). danah boyd (2008c) added layers to Ito's idea by affording them properties similar to those put forward by Johnson:

- replicability – expressions can be copied from one place to another verbatim;
- persistence – communications are recorded for posterity;

- invisible audiences – it can not be fully known who may engage with content in such arenas; and
- searchability – information can be easier to find due to indexing and search facilities.

For sometime then, we have, and continue to, engage with theorisations of digitally mediated publics. Of course, one obvious point of difference between Johnson and boyd's thinking is how each deals with the issue of anonymity and audience. Anonymity in networks featured as an idea in Johnson's work because of the nature of digitally mediated networks (or online communities) at that time – many, though not all, were based on pseudonyms and early thinking in this area often equated pseudonyms with anonymity. In contrast, in recent years we have come to recognise a much higher degree of the use of "real names" in public networks, particularly where SNSs are concerned, and consequently we see boyd implicitly engaging this within her take on networked publics. Johnson's and boyd's positions have resonance today. Anonymity is still possible and pseudonyms are still used – even in spaces such as Facebook, which is often held up as the gold standard when it comes to discourses regarding real name Web practices. Conversely, we also know that even where pseudonyms are used, this should not be conflated with total anonymity (Livia 2002, Hogan 2013). However, like physical space, it is possible to craft private space with digital media as the work of Livia (2002) on use of encrypted pseudonyms on the French public Minitel,[1] Ferreday and Lock (2007) on the development of the tranniesphere, Lange (2007) on the enactment of privately public and publicly private strategies, Papacharissi (2010) viz the potentials of private spheres of interaction and that of Robards (2012) and the continued use of MySpace by young people as a mode of avoiding familial gaze all demonstrate.

I will begin the chapter by considering the processes by which people are introduced to SNSs, how they operate with them in public space and their ethical take on such arrangements. I do this to set the scene for understanding how human actors may, in some respects, have more weight than others in terms of specifying the norms of engagement in such spaces via, for instance, the deployment of moral codes and cultural capital.

Entering SNS publics

As might be expected, and as is shown in other studies (Robards 2012), I found that people generally entered into SNSs because of some kind of prompt from family and friends. For example, as Aleksy said, "the one I first hooked up on was called Grape.pl, it's basically a website, kind of like a prototype of Facebook really, and I got invited by a friend". Aleksy's experience was common, people often spoke of being invited to a site "like Facebook" before actually joining Facebook or another site popular at present such as Twitter. Others mentioned in this vein included Face Party, Hi5 and of course MySpace. As Andy also recalled, "I think the first one that I remember using, my former partner introduced me to, one called Face Party which is quite old school back in the day, about 2002 or something". Old school, interestingly, being only around ten years ago. However, such prompts, or indeed approaches to connect were not always successful, as Xui Li recalled:

> ...my cousins started to use Highfive and they were like, 12, they were really young. It was really funny because they kept asking me at Christmas "Oh, why don't you add me, please add me" and I said no I can't, I don't want to add you because you'll be liking very single photo I post and every single comment I post.
>
> (Xui Li, student, 16–24)

This "failure to connect" was also something mentioned by Wayne who told of how he had joined, and then stopped using, Twitter because:

> people said to me "are you on Twitter, I've tweeted this and that", and I'd no idea what the hash tag thing was, and all of that. But because everyone seems to have a Twitter something, they're twittering away, I thought I'd do it. But I didn't really understand how it worked.
>
> (Wayne, occupational therapist, 45–54)

A further recurring theme was the terms under which people joined – many times people talked of peer pressure either directly: "My friends were on it so they all told me to get on there, so I did" (Sarah), or indirectly "Erm...probably one I first started using was Facebook, and that was primarily because everybody else was using it" (Jyoti). However, it was not just pure peer pressure that facilitated SNS entry. As Wayne said "I wanted to eaves drop and find out what everybody was doing and not be out of the loop." Others talked of specific events in their lives as playing a part. For example, Jenny talked of wanting to view the photographs her brother posted on his year away travelling, Rebecca was living in France at a certain point and saw it as a way to keep in touch with friends and family back in the UK and Ela had recently moved to the UK and eventually used SNSs to maintain a connection with family and friends back in Poland.

Beyond friends and family, others emphasised business as ways into engaging with SNSs: Suzanne, for example, discussed how she had joined Facebook to promote her artwork and Jyoti emphasised the role of LinkedIn for her events management business. Music was another way in for several people who, unsurprisingly, had their first experience with MySpace where a particular band they followed had mentioned taking up a place in that space or they were in a band themselves and had created a profile for it. What I found difficult to find, however, were examples of people who were early adopters – most interviewees seemed to only be able to point to another friend of family member who had introduced them to SNSs. Matt, however, stated that: "I found Twitter. I think through Stephen Fry.[2] I was an early adopter; I had Twitter before everybody else I knew. I used to tell them about it and they'd say " 'oh, what's that?' " Also Kevin identified as an early adopter too:

I'm sort of an early adopter of things, and I'm often one of the first people to try something out, but I don't necessarily use it, I just try it out and then hide it away, and sometimes I come back to it. Like I probably used Facebook before almost everybody I know but I didn't actually then use it for a year or something after that because I just closed it. I couldn't be bothered with it because it was so new and so unpopulated with anybody and it was boring and it was bland and there was nothing going on. It didn't have any of the modern things that it has now so I just couldn't be bothered with that, and thought I'd come back to it in a year when it's a bit better.

(Kevin, sales assistant, 25–34)

Further, related to this idea of who gets into the network first, the timeline for people gaining access was also mentioned, particularly in relation to Facebook:

Somebody told me, one of my friends from home who'd gone to Uni as well, told me that there was this thing called Facebook, but at the time when Facebook first started you had to be a part of the University, and at the time my college, because it was quite small, didn't have Facebook. He was like "Oh it's great, you should get on it", and then finally they let my College onto it so that's when I started using it.

(Hannah, sales assistant, 25–34)

Indeed, it is also perhaps helpful here to remember that not all users gain access to a site at the same time, particularly in its early stages. SNSs can be involved in disconnective practice as they come into being. For example, Facebook featured the well-known staggered roll out via Harvard, the Massachusetts Institute of Technology, the rest of the Ivy League universities, then throughout education institutions in the USA, and other countries before eventually being accessible to the general public. Of course such a strategy is to mitigate risk as owners learn to deal with capacity issues as larger numbers of users join the network, but, additionally, such disconnective practice can be enrolled to create interests and buzz around a set of arrangements as has happened with certain Google products. In addition, several participants told of how their first experience of engaging with SNSs was not necessarily the one that they have now. Entering SNS publics, for these people involved disconnection along the way. Tom, for example, said that it was not until 2010 that he started using it "properly" even though he had an account in place in 2008, because he just did not have a use for it. It was a similar story for Ela:

> I came to the UK on a working summer holiday, and I met some friends, and they said "oh that would be a great way to stay in touch", so I started to set up a profile, and we did use it for that but obviously I only had four friends on it because Facebook, at the time, was not popular in Poland. There was a Polish equivalent that had emerged and everyone was signing up to that instead. But then when I came back to do my degree in 2007, that's when you get to know people, and they had Facebook and started inviting me, and that grew from there.
>
> (Ela, translator, 25–34)

Yet, whereas for Ela and Tom, such disconnection involved not using an account until such time it became relevant for them, Wayne's experience involved him deactivating his account several times before finally engaging with Facebook for the past two years:

> I joined Facebook a few years ago and then quickly deactivated my account because I was worried about what people could see and how it was all shared because I didn't really understand what people could see and what information was out there on me. So I deactivated a few times.
>
> (Wayne, occupational therapist, 45–54)

Moreover, whereas Wayne deactivated his account on his own terms, until he was ready to deal with what he regarded as an confusing set of arrangements, Matt was forced to disconnect by his ex-wife:

> I remember my ex-wife had a complete fit with me being on it. Probably through some fit of jealousy, I had to delete my first Facebook, you know, because she figured I was up to no good, which I wasn't. It was awful, probably her to be honest, but yeah I had to delete it. And obviously we split up and I set it back up again, and it's all fine.
>
> (Matt, train driver, 35–44)

In summary then, whilst I acknowledge that SNSs and networked publics might encourage a particular line of appropriation (boyd 2008c; 2011), or attempt to set the tone for use (Papacharissi 2009), and the role of the "non-human" as detailed in the previous chapter, we should not underestimate the roles of human agency. People enter into SNS publics in a inherently social fashion, one might argue usually via an invitation from someone in their social circle or as a function of social life. It might even be inherently sociotechnical via the enrolment of the invite by email or telephone contact activity offered by many applications. But as I have argued in the previous chapter though, whilst SNSs mediate our activity within such spaces, they do not determine them and I think it is important, even though there features and functions might complicate the lives of people like Wayne (and lead to disconnection), often a re-connection is made because of peer pressure and a need to keep up with people. SNS, I would, and will continue to argue in this chapter, are very much given contexts by use as much as they try to generate a particular set of contexts. These contexts arguably incorporate disconnection alongside connection.

Managing SNS publics – In public

Once within an SNS and outside the boundaries of work and home, there is the question of how one engages with them in physical public space. Such engagements, and the extent to which they are made, can be viewed as interwoven with the content being viewed on the site in question and people's interpretation of the context they find themselves in. This includes privately-public and publicly-private work as demonstrated by prior studies of YouTube (Lange 2007), as Ian describes:

> I am certainly not friends with students on Facebook, and I have my profile as private, so if you were to search for me and find me,

you'd only see my profile picture and my name. You wouldn't be able to log on and see anything else, and my profile page, ... I always have a fairly innocuous profile picture up. A discreet picture up so if someone was searching for me, because there's lots people with my name, but, unless they were friends with me, they wouldn't know it was me because I always cover my face or have a random picture. [in my current profile picture] I'm wearing a scarf on my face, it's stupid. But if a kid wanted to find me they couldn't.

(Ian, school teacher, 35–44)

However, a further mediator here is that of proximity to others and the ability craft a site of disconnection. What I am referring to here is the ability of individuals to make a physical space for themselves to engage with SNS content that gives them a feeling of not being physically overlooked. Here, Hannah gives an example:

I wouldn't go on Facebook if I was on a train and someone was sat next to me because people do look, even if they don't read stuff, they're going to glance. I don't know, I feel it's a bit evasive. In a café, I would, I definitely get stuff out then because it's a bit more private.

(Hannah, sales assistant, 25–34)

In the same way as a café was seen as "more private", people also talked of things such as bus stops and supermarkets as having the same qualities because they could create physical distance between themselves (and more specifically their screen) and other people in that space. Matt even referred to his physical being as a consideration in this respect: "I don't hide the screen or you know, do things like that ... I'm not really bothered about that. No one really tends to look over my shoulder; I'm too tall so it's alright." The parameters of such engagement are also modified by surroundings and content, and by devices. Every participant said that they would generally not use public computers (such as in libraries and cafés), and usually when they did it would be because they were out of the country on holiday or working without access to Wi-Fi or data on a mobile network. It was deemed unnecessary and potentially problematic in that they felt using a public computer offered the best chance of their personal details being stolen or account being hacked. Moreover, Kevin, for instance, said that he did not use his iPad in public because its larger screen would allow people to see what he was doing. He was also worried about his iPad being stolen from him. In fact Xui Li told a story of her friend having her phone stolen from her hand whilst accessing SNSs at a bus stop. These instances bring a more physical notion of safety into the thought put into determining the ability to craft site of disconnection. This goes beyond the safety of a physically private engagement and towards one that is also physically safe. Moreover, there is the question of if such spaces are viewed as appropriate or not.

A number of participants talked about the times at which it was appropriate to engage with SNSs when out in public. This included points made regarding how rude it was to be constantly on your phone checking SNSs whilst at dinner with others. This was seen as antisocial in that SNS use was positioned as having people disconnect with their immediate surroundings, as they engaged with another mode of communication somewhere else. However, there were times this was seen as acceptable – when those who are with you are included in the process of engagement:

> If I'm out with friends on a night out, if something funny has happened, something interesting, I take a picture of it and upload that straight on your phone to Facebook. And I quite like doing that because it's funny. That's how I use it if I'm out and about with friends, take pictures and upload them. That's the only way I do it when I'm outside.
>
> (Bob, cleaner, 25–34)

Another mechanism of appropriate connection was seen whereby participants were out in public on their own, as Bob continued:

> It's kind of an automatic reaction now, if you're stood there for more than 30 seconds and nothing's happening you get your phone out and start playing. That's so notable with a vast amount of people that if you're in a crowd, at least 60% of them will be looking at their phones.
>
> (Bob, cleaner, 25–34)

For many participants such activity, as Bob describes above, would be centred on checking up on what others were doing, letting others know what they were doing or sharing content – particularly funny photos people had taken of things they had seen in public space. Simon particularly noted that on the move it would be more about him signalling his activity to others rather than connecting directly, the latter activity he described as being within the purview of his SNS activity when back home. Kerry operated in a similar fashion too stating that she usually engaged in what she saw as direct connection when at home:

> ...if somebody asks something or somebody's put something, then I feel the need to answer I'll just do that, but whereas when I'm at home I'll probably comment on things that I wouldn't comment on when I'm out and about. See what I mean? So I think it's a bit different when I've got a bit more time when I'm at home.
>
> (Kerry, local government worker, 35–44)

Public ethics

When I developed the interview protocol for this study, it was first late in 2012 and then revised in 2013, when the interviews were conducted. By this time there had been much discussion in the UK, and press internationally for that matter, regarding the various ethical problems that were emerging for people using such spaces. I therefore felt that interviewees would readily respond to a general, very broad question around what people thought the ethical issues were. In fact, this was one of the questions that people really struggled to answer because it was so broad – people were overwhelmed by their own awareness of the issues in this area. A common response was – "Wow that's a really difficult one." Once given starting examples, participants were able to articulate wide-ranging views on the nature of ethical public behaviours with SNSs ranging from the descriptive to the normative in nature. A first area of discussion was the nature of posts made within sites and the associated moral obligations, as Daphne and Nina articulated:

> you shouldn't be having a go at people that...you shouldn't be bringing your bigotry online. If that would be a way of putting it?.. And legally, you can be done for what you do online, you should be aware of it. People have been.
>
> (Daphne, local councillor, 65+)

> I would say, personally, an issue that I have with social networking and ethics and law is, I don't know if you've ever come across these things on Facebook that are called the Lad Bible and stuff like that? Anyway, it's this page where people would post unsavoury things, basically horrible things like rape jokes, racist jokes, just horrible things, and that is just allowed to be on Facebook. So I would say that

is a political issue of freedom of speech, that's an on going argument, should people be allowed to tweet racist things constantly.

(Nina, sales assistant, 16–24)

I chose to use quotes from Daphne and Nina here, not just because they emphasise elements of descriptive and normative ethical positions, but also because of their diverse ages. Nina was one of the youngest participants in the study and Daphne was the oldest yet they share much in common in terms of their fundamental positions regarding ethically acceptable public behaviour and I think it is important given that much research into age and the Internet, and SNSs in particular, emphasises age as a mode of differentiation. Whist I acknowledge this can be this case, and that this can have disconnective effects, I think it is important to note shared understandings. A slightly different take on posting and ethics, more in terms of harm, was presented by Tom. He was very angry at stumbling across a video which purported to show the beheading of someone:

That disturbed me; I couldn't move for about an hour. It were somewhere in the Middle East. Cut his fingers off then cut his head off. There was no censoring on it; people posted it for likes. There needs to be some sort of control. Disgusting.

(Tom, retail assistant, 16–24)

Others took the effects of SNSs in terms of ethics into a related domain, beyond the need not to post what was seen as ethically questionable materials, and towards the idea that SNSs might actually shape our ethics in what they saw as potentially positive ways. For example, Aleksy pointed out it was more difficult to lie to friends now as others might tell a different version of events on SNSs and put you in a difficult position. Kevin also pointed to how the nature of SNSs also potentially shaped what was deemed to be publicly acceptable discourse:

... if I posted something on Facebook which was, "God I hate fat people", I would fully expect my friends to say to me "you can't say that", they would, together, enforce an informal ethical boundary on me. But if I was to say "I want to kill fat people", I could fully expect the police to knock on my door and say "this has been reported to us and we consider this a crime".

(Kevin, sales assistant, 25–34)

During discussions regarding ethics, legal issues were also brought to the fore, as in the case of Kevin above. Of course legal issues are not necessarily ethical issues and vice versa, but participants did link the two. For example, the question of whether it was right for legal proceedings to be brought against people for postings they made in SNSs was a key area. Several participants noted the presence of various police forces within SNSs and how they engaged with them for identifying and solving crimes or activity deemed to be criminal. In particular, authorities were seen as not acting in a legitimate way, and being heavy handed when people, for example posted updates that the participants felt were clearly not meant to be taken seriously. Aleksy and Ian for instance both were critical of people having been arrested by the police for saying they were going to "blow up" an airport. As Kevin expanded:

> I think there is, potentially, a place for it but, I mean, I don't think it's always necessarily right to act on everything, they perhaps act on things too, like somebody the other day had a knock on from the police and the police told them that they had been trying to track them down for four weeks and had done a major investigation on them because they said they would like to egg the Prime Minister on Facebook. Likewise when the person who said he was going to bomb the airport because his flight was delayed. I think there is a tendency to take things out of context which I think, if you go down that route of taking everything that somebody says, on the internet, as a genuine threat, it's just madness. It's like pre-crime, it's like some Orwellian thing where whatever somebody thinks, says, is judged as a potential crime, that doesn't work, that's not reality.
>
> (Kevin, sales assistant, 25–34)

Another area discussed in legal terms related to the potentially libellous nature of SNSs where several participants, including Jyoti and Ian, raised the case of the late Conservative Peer Lord McAlpine who was wrongly accused, via Twitter, of being a paedophile after a BBC Newsnight investigation, and subsequently sued comedian Alan Davis and political activist Sally Bercow, who had both sent defamatory tweets (Sweney 2013a, 2013b, 2013c). Other participants also talked about the stories they had heard of, or seen in the news, regarding violent threats against friends and partners, hate crimes, the incitement of violence and, of course, cyber bullying and threats from paedophiles. When asked directly who was responsible for maintaining ethical order in such spaces participants generally pointed to the users of SNSs and the owners of the site in question – or rather more specifically – reified abstractions of the owners. For example, people would state that Facebook or Twitter should do something about it.

> Steve whatever his name is from Facebook. Facebook definitely, they presumably are responsible for the settings or how the system works or how easy it is to navigate and how intuitive it is. So yeah, Facebook. Not me. Definitely not me.
>
> (Jyoti, sales director, 35–44)

> The person who designed it! The person who designed it, because the person who's programmed it is probably a different person. It's the designer's fault. Yeah.
>
> (Kerry, local government worker, 35–44)

It was only upon further prompting and discussion that participants recognised the role of the SNS software as, for example, being implicated ethically whereby participants recognised the role of it in affording anonymity (even with the so called real name Web) or through the potential for it to generate context collisions. However, ultimately, as Jyoti and Kerry point out, the non-human was eschewed in favour of pointing the finger at someone rather than something.

Regulating publics I – No sex please, we're British!

It has been argued that social norms appear to both limit (Davis 2012), and expand (Van Doorn 2010), the range of identities that one can express in a particular online context. It is also the case that SNSs exhibit processes that can create, control and monitor new public spaces through the architecture of the network itself (Mejias 2010) and indeed their philosophy (see Chapter 2). Consequently I think it is important to understand what activites are regarded as not for public consumption, or only under very particular terms. Therefore, participants were asked if there were parts of their lives they wouldn't share via SNSs or things they would do with SNSs they would not tell other people about. Without prompting, everyone said that they had nothing to hide, and keeping things back from others was not something they would do. A couple of participants very briefly referred to incidents involving recreational drug use where they had been photographed smoking marijuana and had found it necessary to have this content removed, but most went on to speak instead of issues of sex and sexuality. Both men and women in this group asked if pornography was being referred to, and that if it was, then yes they watched it, but it was not something they felt they had to hide. If they were asked by anyone if they watched it they would tell them, but they would not share that kind of material in SNSs because they felt it was not appropriate to do so. To qualify this, the SNS people were referring to here included mainstream sites such as Facebook, Twitter and Instagram. Additionally, users of what might be seen as sexually charged sites with SNS functionalities, such as Fitlads and Gaydar, recognised the potential for pornographic image sharing in those spaces, but also said that it would not be something that they would generally connect with mainstream sites – again because it was not seen as an appropriate connection. This discussion of pornography blurred into the circulation of sexual imagery with SNSs more generally. Nina for example, provided an account of her experiences at school:

> ...when we were at school, this girl sent a naked picture of herself to this boy at my school on Facebook, and it got put on Facebook by loads of different people and everyone school got in serious legal trouble for possessing child pornography because we were under 18 and that is classed as child pornography even if it is taken by children for the use of children or whatever. Still, but it was bad. Everyone got their phones confiscated and the police came and stuff, not me, I wasn't involved. ... the girl was pretty devastated, obviously. I think some of the boys got their phones taken off them and a serious warning from the police...
>
> (Nina, sales assistant, 16–24)

Beyond this, the gay male participants in particular expressed a desire to disconnect the more sexually explicit aspects of their SNS activity, and social networking activity more generally undertaken in these spaces, and make it distinct from their mainstream activities. Wayne, for example, was particularly keen to maintain such a distinction:

> I wouldn't tell everybody, for example, that I used a Gaydar account because they don't need to know that. Not that it's a secret, it just isn't appropriate to tell them. ... I don't like people to know my business, particularly, I don't always like them to know my sexuality, so if I told them I was on that site, then they'd know wouldn't they, I suppose. It's just not something I would talk about, I would chat to people on there of course, I'm happy to do that, but I wouldn't tell everybody I was on it. ... I wouldn't hide it from anyone. Say if

someone wanted to borrow my laptop and then they realised that
I was on that site because if they found out I'd been using the site
because they can do something clever with the laptop, it wouldn't
be that I was hiding it, it would just be that perhaps I just wouldn't
mention it . . . because the Facebook site is anybody and everybody,
whereas that one isn't, it's more of a discreet line out, I suppose, it's
kind of a lifestyle things rather than an everywhere social thing.

(Wayne, occupational therapist, 45–54)

Similarly, Andy stated that the site he used had an explicit tagline,
something like, "for guys that are admirers of guys" and he did not
want that site connecting with his mainstream activity as he wanted
to keep that part of his life compartmentalised. Specifically, he was concerned that he was friends with his 12-year-old nephew on Facebook and
stated that "I wouldn't want my nephew to see, I don't have anything
dodgy on there, I genuinely don't, but I still wouldn't want my nephew
going 'uncle, what's this about'". However, Andy did note that he had
seen other people posting pictures of men wearing very little clothing.
Indeed, Jason spoke of how one of his posts which he described as being
"a bit lewd" had led to his cousin chastising him via a message that
read "just to let you know that I actually sit in front of the computer
with my daughters" and the subsequent deletion of her connection
with him within Facebook. It is not only disconnective practice as self-
censorship that is enrolled in relation to notions of decency within
SNSs, disconnective practice may be taken against others to craft a public space that conforms to their expectations of acceptable behaviour.
Interestingly, Jason was very considered in his discussion of sex, sexuality and pornography as related to SNSs more generally. For instance,
he set out particular rules for himself in terms of what he would access
and where. He reported that he would access Fitlads in say a café, but
only if he could see there was only adults around – he felt adults could
take care of themselves and if they were offended that was their problem, not his. However, he would not access such content at his site of
voluntary work as that was not appropriate because he was supposed
to be paying attention to what he was doing. In the case of his cousin,
Jason had connected with her as an adult and was not expecting her
to give her children access to his profile – he only had adult friends.
In contrast to studies of email then, which posit the regulatory potential,
and specifically compliance, brought about by copying in (Skovholt and
Svennevig 2006), here the copying in of Jason's cousin (and her daugh-
ter), led to a destabilisation of the regulated environment his cousin was

trying to construct and she did not "comply". Instead, she engaged in disconnective practice in an attempt to maintain her regulated environment. This case illustrates how disconnective practice may be facilitated by the construction of imagined audience (Marwick and boyd 2011b) or rooted in a lack of knowledge of hidden audiences (boyd 2008c, 2008b, 2011) and potential bystanders (Ferneley and Light 2008). Moreover, what we see here is how the nature of a space might influence thought regarding the extent to which one might connect them. The spaces these men used, in addition to hooking up, were engaged to maintain long-term close platonic relationships. Although other studies have demonstrated that as relationships become stronger between people, they begin to display media multiplexity (Haythornthwaite 2005), here it seems to be not so clear cut. To clarify, the idea of media multiplexity refers to the conduct of relationships through increasing numbers of media as those relationships become stronger and closer. What I interpreted, was that some of these men would restrict their use of media for this set of relationships to one media, even though they had access to others. Wayne, in particular, is good example of this. The development of media multiplexity therefore might be challenged by a desire not to connect in order to maintain spaces as for specific purposes and disconnective practice is integral to this. Importantly, I do not see such a challenge as restricted to gay men, one might consider a range of groups or individuals who wish to develop a strong relationship via one medium. Examples here might include those engaged in extra-relationship affairs, arenas for the provision of support for domestic violence victims and those with certain long-term health conditions.

The participants in this study discussed differing levels of engagement with sexually explicit materials as related to SNSs and, generally, it was clear that they felt it was not appropriate to connect such activity publicly. I therefore was interested to explore the extent to which the exploration for new sexual and/or romantic partners might figure in such spaces given that such searches are usually a public matter in the sense that meeting partners and the process of dating is often happens in public space. If SNSs are experienced as and with public space then, what role is there, if any, for meeting partners in these spaces? SNSs do offer opportunities for finding partners whether this is a specific element of functionality added, as in sites such as Fit Lads or apps such as Tinder or via their capacity for such forms of sociality and socialisation to take place. Katie, Rebecca and Xui Li, for instance, all met partners via SNSs. For Rebecca and Xui Li, however, they already had some knowledge of the person in question – both had known their partners as children and had reconnected. Rebecca's husband, a friend from when they were at school, approached her via Facebook and Xui Li was approached by the son of her parents' accountant via Hi5 – they too had known each other from the age of 6. Katie, who met her partner via Flickr had no knowledge of him prior to that. Conversely, a number of stories emerged in which SNSs had, when people were new to them, been seen as dating sites and this had caused relationship problems:

> ... my stepsister, when she first got her Facebook account, it caused a bit of a rift in their marriage. Her husband really thought that she was being a slag basically, just engaging in relationships with strangers, he didn't quite understand that she just saw it as something that was a piece of fun, but he really saw it as a problem within the relationship. I think its something that he's very slowly just come to terms with but for a long time it just was one of the nails in the coffin that nearly actually ruined their marriage, they nearly got divorced at one point. I don't think it was all over Facebook but I think that was an extremely large contributing factor.
>
> (Jason, unemployed/charity volunteer, 25–34)

Even though SNSs have allowed people to make sexual and romantic relationships, and they can cause problems for sexual and romantic relationships, there were a range of views regarding the extent participants would engage in this, who they would tell and how they felt about others who chose to. Kevin, for instance, wondered if experiencing a friend's engagement might affect his perception of them: "you can't help but feel slightly different about somebody if you know their intimate sexual fetishes" and Sarah thought it would be weird to meet people via the Internet, but overall participants felt it was okay for other people to date via SNSs and connect their SNS accounts with any external dating site they might be using. Regarding themselves, several reported using sites specifically geared towards dating only (such as Match.com and eHarmony) and others said they would use them. For this kind of site, participants said they would be open about their usage. However, although participants stated that they would not mind others doing this, everyone said they would not connect any dating account they had with their SNSs, even though they were aware some sites offered this feature. This was not because they were embarrassed about using a dating site, it was because they felt it was not an appropriate connection to make (for them) in an SNS space. Nina, for example, stated that is would involve publicising her private life too much and did not like the idea of people seeing that she had gone on a failed blind date with a woman, Jyoti did not want people at work knowing about her personal life in that respect and Xui Li was worried about family interventions:

> If I was single and went on a dating site and logged on Facebook I don't really want to post, yeah Xui Li had logged on to dating site, Xui Li is going on a date with so and so and at this time. I know my relatives quite well, they'd check on me on the date "Oh, going well?" [Laughs] "Ooh, she's going to the Trafford centre on a date, let's go to the Trafford centre, family trip!"
>
> (Xui Li, student, 16–24)

Interestingly, although it has been argued that the basic issue in respect of online connection to sexual content and access to partners is that it equates to increased personal or professional trouble via "fast connections" (Weiss and Samenow 2010), my participants seemed more concerned with issues of privacy and relevance rather than getting into some kind of trouble. Of course, I do not dismiss getting into trouble as a reason for why some people might engage in disconnective practice regarding sex and sexual relationships. I also do not assume that others would not engage in revealing much that is private about themselves in order to attract a partner via SNSs. As another study reports on a participant, Bijan, who used his profile to showcase his nearly naked physical body and receive validations from women that he is sexy (Manago 2013).

Case study: Classical music audiences and their disconnection with SNSs

A second area I want to raise regarding the role of disconnection in regulating publics relates to the role of particular cultures. Here I will draw on published joint work I was involved with relating to the development of an SNS-enabled app for a UK-based symphony orchestra (Crawford et al. 2014). The Student Mobile Project involved the development of an app that could take advantage of the SNS participation of a UK symphony orchestra's existing student audience. The point was to sell discounted tickets to a student audience in a more cost-effective way, improve levels of interaction between the symphony orchestra and their audience and use the SNS participation of existing audiences to expand its audience. In terms of increasing ticket sales, the app was successful. However, the extent of connection possible via the enrolment of audience SNS participation was not realised.

The event details page of the app provides links to Facebook, Twitter and email. This allows the consumer to construct an email indicating that they are looking at this event or publish a similar message to Facebook or Twitter. However, only one of the participants in the focus groups indicated that they had used the links to SNSs and all believed that their use during a concert, even to augment proceedings, should not be allowed. Nevertheless, comments, about the app being "handy", were quite typical. Every focus group participant who commented indicated that they were almost never without their mobile phone, and therefore having an app that allowed them to purchase tickets was really convenient. Hence, it seemed that the app and the students' mobile phones played an important symbolic role in maintaining connectedness to the orchestra.

However, focus group participants were generally pessimistic that the app could be used to necessarily attract a new audience, unfamiliar with classical music. Of those surveyed in this research 83% indicated that they had previously attended at least one other classical music concert in the previous 12 months. And in the focus groups only two (from 81) indicated that they had never been to a classical music concert before; and neither indicated that the app had played any significant role in them attending. The researchers in this study identified a discourse of complexity surrounding classical music, how it is learnt and the need for it to be hard work. Most participants reported that they began engaging with classical music at a very early age, being introduced to it predominantly by family members. The participants reported they would have difficulty in explaining how they would "teach someone" who had not grown up with classical music and many doubted it was possible.

Therefore, whilst SNSs may offer opportunities for engaging known and unknown audiences via the spreading and searching of persistent information related to user activity, this is not predetermined. In a classical music context, the data from this study suggests that even where data from the app is shared via SNSs, the engagement of those without a history of attending concerts is perceived to be of limited potential. The participants indicated that they would not use the app to invite the previously uninitiated where it came to classical music and instead would aim to restrict the spreading of information throughout SNSs to those who knew about classical music culture already. Importantly, even if someone who had never been to a classical music event saw information about a concert attendance posted, the study participants reported they would have difficulty in engaging them because classical music was something they perceived as being difficult to educate people about (even though they themselves had learnt it, and usually at a very early age).

In this case classical music culture is a key set of arrangements that work against the enrolment of SNS for audience expansion. In fact, the authors demonstrate that those engaged with classical music culture in their study engaged with SNSs in a way that reinforces structural arrangements in this area. Participation with classical music is deemed as suitable for only for those with prior knowledge and even though any postings about a concert had the potential to be read by those new to the culture, classical music culture dominates, audience expansion is perceived to be problematic and disconnection occurs. In the same way as boyd (2012) discusses "white flight" in SNSs, one sees class and culture being enrolled here in terms of disconnection.

Conclusion

Whilst people take cues from others within a network in relation to what to present, other things are also at play including non-human actors and a complex set of power dynamics involving our agency and personal structures. This chapter demonstrates how such power dynamics are implicated in how we enter SNSs and also how disconnection may play a part along the way.

Once in SNSs, there are questions regarding how these can be engaged with in public space. The participants in the study demonstrate how disconnective practice can be important here. Engaging with SNSs in public space can involve the crafting spaces that are beyond the physical gaze of others by taking account of furniture, proximity, bodies and devices. Moreover, such disconnection is perceived as important not only to craft private spaces, but also create spaces that are safe also. Notions of safety then can affect our connective and disconnective practice. In this chapter, I also demonstrate how acceptable behaviours may fuel our desires to connect or disconnect as participants mention how manners and ethics are important. Interestingly, when asked about an open question about what is not shared in public, universally everyone said they had nothing to hide, yet most went on to mention sex and pornography as something not to be shared in mainstream spaces. SNSs then are regulated by a notion of "common standards of decency" but also, as the case of UK symphony orchestra demonstrates; other ideological positions may come into play too depending upon the situation. Ultimately then I argue, disconnective practice can be influential in the creation and regulation of publics.

5
Navigating Work

Introduction

When you talk with people about the link between SNSs and work, often the discussion centres on whether or not they should be used at work and problems of clashes between personal and work life. This issue of collapse of contexts is often mentioned in the literature, particularly as related to discussions about the presentation of self (boyd 2006, DiMicco and David 2007, Kendall 2007). Of course collapse of contexts is not something restricted to work, as boyd and Kendall would be quick to point out. Moreover, such collapse of contexts generally, and in relation to work, pre-date SNSs. For example, prior to the Industrial Revolution, it was common for work to be undertaken at home. Home was work, and work was home, for those engaging in the cottage industries. Indeed, it is helpful here to highlight that today, such arrangements exist across both developed and developing economic contexts. The blurring of contemporary home and work is not restricted to cottage industries or farming; for example, developments in information and communication technologies have facilitated the rise of home-based working for certain occupational groups. The debate regarding the boundary between home and work continues and has to some extent been amplified by the pervasiveness of SNSs for many people. I believe that SNSs have done two key things in this respect. They have blurred the lines between work arrangements and home arrangements, and they have expanded the number of people engaging with work arrangements and home arrangements via digital media and the Internet. What I mean by this is that SNSs have become an additional digital arrangement by which work activity might take place. The participants in this study, for example, undertook information-sharing activity, arranged shift cover, sourced advice and, unsurprisingly, created networking possibilities with these arrangements. They may not always have considered these arrangements as work oriented, but work activity clearly happens with them. Moreover, such activity was not limited to SNSs such as LinkedIn. In addition, I think we can agree that more people are now using the Internet in a personal capacity, and such modes that go beyond online shopping and banking. SNSs, I would argue, and I think many would agree, have opened the door of online sociality to a much greater number and broader range of people than earlier forms of Internet-facilitated sociality did. The combined effect of this, I think, is that we have a greater number and diversity of people engaging with work via the Internet. Despite the obvious marketing efforts of sites such as LinkedIn, digital networks are being used, in relation to work, by a range of people beyond those that might be seen as holding professional roles. Perhaps this is due to the fact that people are now realising that the performance of connectedness has become a contemporary indicator of employability (Gregg 2009) and that informal networking improves job seekers chances of securing a position they want (Van Hoye et al. 2009). Hence, as Clark and Roberts (2010) propose, while employers have always been able to request background and reference information on job applicants, they have reserved this for particular kinds of post due to the associated costs and legal requirements. This position is changing now, whereby greater ranges of people are searched online, usually without their knowledge.

Alongside these developments then is research and commentary which, for instance, interrogates the value of SNSs for organisations in terms of their abilities to facilitate collaboration and remote working (DiMicco and David 2007), recruitment (Smith and Kidder 2010, Brown and Vaughn 2011); employee surveillance (Kaupins and Park 2011) and product and service marketing (Barnes and Barnes 2009). However, such engagements are not unproblematic as the legal status of content posted within SNSs can vary between countries (Davies and Lee 2008, Baughman 2010) as do privacy laws (Clark and Roberts 2010). Therefore, it has been argued that, if used in selection processes, data posted with SNSs might be seen to contravene equal opportunity policies (Smith and Kidder 2010). Photographs and age data posted with SNSs might contain information used to discriminate, for instance. There are also more general ethical questions regarding the rights of employers to interrogate the private lives of employees or potential employees, especially where the information posted with SNSs might be inaccurate, unbalanced and irrelevant (Kaupins and Park 2011). Kaupins and Park also point to other ethical and legal problems in relation to the extent to which it is an employer's obligation tackle bullying and harassment occurring amongst employees on SNSs, and to ensure that friending practices are consistent amongst managers in order that favouritism is not enacted. In the interviews conducted for this study, the problems people experienced, or were aware of regarding other people, were recounted and as can be seen to very much fall into line with what we already know (see examples in Table 5.1). In this chapter, I go beyond descriptions, and

Table 5.1   Examples of work oriented SNS problems

My friend was off sick with a bad back, but while she was off she was a arranging a birthday night out. She's already been given a date to return to work which was before her night out and a couple of people were mad because she was arranging nights out while she was off sick. But she was arranging a night out for when she'd come back to work anyway. You know, for a month later, and she got really slagged off at work; really slated at work by management. So yeah, you need to be really careful, especially if you're off sick and putting comments on Facebook. (Julie, health care assistant, 35–44)
I teach at a girls' school and one of the big networking sites that the teenagers used at the time was Bebo. A load of girls that I taught had surreptitiously been taking photographs of me while I was teaching; I was totally unaware of this. They had been posting, they had created a false account under my name and they had posted a load of photographs of me up on this site, as though this was me. Then they had all decided to comment and write various comments on photographs, about myself, erm, and unbeknown to me, this went on for about a month before I overheard a girl . . . no, a girl came up to me in a lesson and she said "Oh, hi Sir, I like your Bebo page". And I, at that point I didn't even know what Bebo was; I hadn't heard of it. So obviously pursued this and she said you've got a Bebo page and these photographs up. I said no I haven't, I don't know about this, tell me more, and we got to the bottom of it, this thing being set up . . . Yeah, the comments were inappropriate, shall we say. They were of . . . yeah, they were young teenager girls being silly and making inappropriate comments about me as a teacher. Of a sexual nature. So, I then informed one of the more senior teachers of the school, who then pulled all of these students together and basically gave them 24 hours to remove the site and it was removed. That was the end of it. (Ian, school teacher, 35–44)

remedies for SNS-related difficulties people experience regarding work. In this chapter I am predominantly interested in how people navigate SNSs in relation to work through the enrolment of selective connectivity and more specifically disconnective practice.

Linking work and the personal

During the interviews the most popular response to questioning around the extent to which personal and work lives were connected related to friending practices. Almost everyone said that they only connected, via what they considered to be personal SNS spaces, with colleagues at work if they became friends outside work. However, this was not the case for everyone; Julie, for example, stated that about half of her 200 friends on Facebook were current or ex-colleagues. Where relevant to the participant in question, some reported connecting with colleagues to what they saw as their work spaces, such as LinkedIn or Twitter. Within the participants in this study, there was also a dominant view that supervisors and managers were not the right kind of people to connect with; Ian's comments below reflect the typical sentiment expressed by these people:

> Yes, but I'm very particular about which colleagues I am friends with because I treat Facebook as a social forum. For me it's not a professional thing. I will write silly things in there and sometimes rude things or whatever, so the colleagues that I have on Facebook aren't very particular about who they are...I'm not friends with anyone on Facebook that is senior to me at work, put it that way. Because I don't want them...and if they ever try to add me as a friend I try to ignore them, because I don't want to be connected with them in a kind of social sense...I don't want them to know what I get up to on the weekends, basically. It's none of their business.
>
> (Ian, school teacher, 35–44)

One exception in particular was Matt who did connect with supervisors and management:

> I know there's a few people who won't be friends with, like, people in management because they think they're spying, but I don't have that problem. I'm friends with management, it doesn't bother me. Must be people who are up to no good that don't like it, so...
>
> (Matt, train driver, 35–44)

It perhaps would be easy to explain these two positions as concerned with the different work roles that Ian and Matt have, and indeed I believe this does have some affect on disconnective practice as I shall expand on later in this chapter. However, there is more at work here. The narrative Ian presents, also points to a desire to be able to operate with SNSs without being monitored by your supervisor or manager, because as Ian puts it, "it's none of their business". This sentiment of choosing not to connect in an attempt to keep aspects of personal life, personal, was a strong feature of such discussions, irrespective of role at work. Such reasoning also extended to rationales for choosing not to connect multiple SNSs together, where work was deemed to be for one space or only certain spaces and that seen as personal for another or others. For Jyoti, this also meant that personal contacts should not be present in professional networks:

> Yeah, I had er, erm, a LinkedIn um ... invitation from somebody that I know, that's my husband's step-sister which I haven't accepted basically, because as far as I'm concerned LinkedIn is very work-related. It just doesn't to me make sense to be linked with friends on LinkedIn.
>
> (Jyoti, sales director, 35–44)

The experiences of the participants in this study are different to those reported in others, where it has been argued that many users will try to synchronise their profiles on Facebook and LinkedIn (van Dijck 2013c). That said, the extent to which personal activity and work were separate, and separated, was contested. Andy felt that, potentially, if you were doing illegal things online and were tagged as working for a particular employer, then they could argue that you were bringing the company into disrepute:

> Again, it depends on who posts it as well because if you put something on, if you're doing something illegal, and you're sharing it, then I think they should be entitled to say if it's illegal, it's damaging to the company. I know that's it article 8, the right to private life and you should be allowed that but if it is damaging. I think to a certain extent as well, it depends whether you put yourself out to your employer but yes, you do give your work details out on these, not everyone does but some people's profiles would say "works at such a place", but in that situation, for example Jack Whitehall, wasn't he photographed snorting cocaine? So if there was a picture of me

doing that and beneath it is said "works for the Cooperative Group", I think they'd have quite a good case for gross misconduct in that it would damage the reputation of the company and I think they could probably use that even if I posted it and they don't own the image.

(Andy, legal professional, 25–34)

Indeed, others also pointed to the potential openness of SNSs and how this might afford employers certain rights under certain conditions. Jacob, Jyoti and Matt all took the position that if a person was going to have an SNS account, and left it open, they could not complain if work colleagues, supervisors and managers looked at this and made judgments about them, or took action against them. Further, for this reason, some participants spoke of engaging in disconnective practice to edit their online presence retrospectively and for the future:

I retreated for 6 months and just lay low for a bit, till I'd consolidated who I wanted to be, and I basically went with my professional self...I also focused much more on my professional platforms and over time my use of the play platforms has really fallen off and I mainly use things professionally.

(Katie, social technologist, 35–44)

Interestingly Andy was one of these people too:

I think there a couple of pictures from years ago which were on there which I had to untag where I was smoking marijuana, obviously I don't want work people to know that so I had to untag those.

(Andy, legal professional, 25–34)

The points the participants make here are underpinned by a belief that, for them, it is difficult for people to complain when things are posted openly – some even said that people deserved to be picked up on things if they were stupid enough to leave things open. Yet, all these people still expected to be able to undertake personal activities with SNSs that fell outside the gaze of work. Such discussions speak to other previous work in relation to SNSs where Papacharissi (2010) discusses the requirements for "redactional acumen" and indeed earlier work regarding online communication which acknowledges the issues associated with historical activities becoming a contemporary problem (Rice and Love 1987).

Talking about work

Whether or not people connect with those they associate with at work in personal spaces, a further point of connection and disconnection is present. This point is concerned with the act of talking about work in personal spaces. Several participants engaged in disconnective practice in this area by not talking about work at all, in what they interpreted as personal spaces. Although some did and in a very direct way:

> I don't really like working that much, so if I do post a status at work, if I'm on there I'm usually a little bit ticked off and kind of rant about being at work in this god-awful, you know, or wish I was at home.
>
> (Bob, cleaner, 25–34)

> I stopped swearing in March 2010, I stopped swearing on Twitter, and that was a conscious thing because I was being put forward for this award and basically the case for the award went in and then the [awarding body] started following me and all of a sudden I thought "oh shit" so I stopped swearing on Twitter that day, I found it quite hard at first but I'm used to it now and now I feel a bit weird about swearing on Twitter. So what I do now, if I'm feeling really sweary, and lots of people know I do this and they find it really funny, I do what I call time release tweet and I'll just go "fucking . . . ." and then after 10 seconds I will delete it so it's not enough time for Google to pick it up, but I still get the satisfaction of having that swearing rant. So that's my tactic now. Yes, and I'll actually say "this is only going to be here for 10 seconds" sometimes, and it's dead funny because sometimes my followers will try and screen grab them and be like "yeah". So I just make a bit of a game about it.
>
> (Katie, social technologist, 35–44)

The example Katie provides is particularly interesting as it was not her employer that modified her behaviour in relation to talking directly about work and using expletives, it was her own self-censorship and the idea of not being recognised in her work that affected her practice. Katie's example is also a good illustration of how disconnective practice might be used playfully in a professional/work context in order to have others engage with from within a network. However, other participants were more indirect, and deployed disconnective strategies in an attempt to allow them to speak freely without any adverse response. Simon, for instance, reported being very vague in his status updates if he wanted to talk about problems. Aleksy, in contrast, said what he felt but used a different language:

> I got in trouble once for fixing something I wasn't supposed to, and I got really upset about that because at the end of the day I actually helped this person who had really big problems doing whatever they were doing. And I got told off for it, and I complained about it on Facebook and I complained in Polish and obviously nobody at work speaks Polish. So a mate of mine picked it up straight away and I explained what this was and what that was, and we started talking on Facebook and I found out that on that day, because I had left early, people at work were actually looking up what I'd written on Google Translate just to work out what I was complaining about.
>
> (Aleksy, IT analyst, 25–34)

A further strategy was deployed by Daphne involving recontextualisation work:

> I'm always scared that something that you put on Facebook could be more public than you want it to be, so I always work on the basis that everyone can see everything. In which case I don't come out with "that so-and-so...". Yes, it would be a more restrained comment that...I might say the same thing but in a way that can't be told that you've called him every name under the sun. No, I come out with line like "I'm looking forward to having the sort of class sizes David Cameron keeps telling me he had at school – roll on the day when we have the same class sizes as at Eton", you know. It's just another way of doing it, but I wouldn't ask, I'm always concerned that people can see it and people might say it's a private account... so many people put their foot in it. I've got a pair of size 8's which are quite capable of.... So I'm careful.
>
> (Daphne, local councillor, 65+)

These examples demonstrate how disconnective practice can be enrolled in a variety of ways to allow people to speak about work-related issues. Going beyond the approach of not connecting with colleagues, these strategies seek to afford disconnection by providing "linguistic cover" through the deployment of language to engage in a politic of softening meaning for certain audiences or making it more difficult to decipher. Such strategies, of course, are not bound to provide the cover the person using them seeks as other actors, human and non-human, come into play to facilitate the interpretation of the meanings presented. This is particularly well demonstrated in the case Aleksy discusses above. This form of disconnective practice, I think, adds to the more visually and identity-oriented ways of engaging in privately public and publicly private strategies put forward by Lange (2007). Moreover, the participants' experiences I report here resonate with other work which highlights the potentials for linguistic resistance within SNSs. Cunliffe (2009), for instance, signals how the Welsh language has been used in a range of SNSs including YouTube, Flickr and MySpace. Flickr in particular is given as an example whereby users collect examples of poorly translated Welsh-language signs in an attempt to affect remedial action.

Employers and disconnection

So far, I have emphasised disconnective practice with SNSs as related to work in relation to employees. In this section, I will emphasise the role that employers can place in affecting employee abilities to connect with SNSs. My argument is that employers can facilitate and dictate modes of disconnective practice.

The first way the participants in this study talked of how employers mandated disconnection with SNSs at work was via the deployment of organisational policy. Such policies involved blanket prescriptions regarding non-use of SNSs involving organisationally owned technology, even during employee breaks and lunch hours (but not always). Some even went so far as to dictate non-use of SNSs via employee-owned devices, such as mobile phones. Here, Sarah (a call centre worker) told of how she could get a warning if she was seen even to have her phone on her desk and Tom (a retail assistant) spoke of how he had to keep his phone in his locker at work. Others spoke of not being able to discuss work with SNSs for data protection or confidentiality reasons. Rebecca (a school teacher) and Simon (a civil servant who worked in a tribunal setting) are examples here. What we can see here, is that to some extent, the nature of the work that these people are doing is influencing organisational policy and the extent to which employees can connect with SNSs as related to work. The question of the extent to which such attempts and dictates by employers to control employees at work, and outside of it, is desirable or effective is a complicated one to answer as it depends on so many factors. What is clear is that, in the case of my participants at least, and in the literature (Kaupins and Park 2011), some employers are deploying overly simplistic policies which incorporate an inherent distrust in the abilities of the people that work for them to engage appropriately in disconnective practice.

The latter point is resonant with the second means by which some employers engage in disconnective practice – though the technical blocking of SNSs use within the organisation. Such an approach was also combined with a policy on use/non-use on a number of occasions. Such blocking, however, was pointed out to be contradictory by some participants. Andy, for instance, told of how his employer would point everyone to the new social media campaign they were running, but yet no one could access it at work. Simon discussed the contradictions surrounding the types of site that were available to be accessed whereby the organisation's position was that work computers were for business only and this was a reason for not allowing access to SNSs but yet, over lunch it was deemed to be acceptable to use a range of other personal sites, such as the BBC and eBay. Jenny also discussed how there was "super lock down" at the school were she worked, for both staff and students, yet for some reason the school seemed not to have taken account of the fact that students and staff might have smartphones.

In another case, Julie told of how SNSs were banned because of organisational bullying taking place within them:

> No, you can't. Facebook's banned. They've blocked it so you can't access Facebook at all at work on their computers, because there was some bullying going on and it was really hard to police because it was all on Facebook. So they just banned it.
>
> (Julie, health care assistant, 35–44)

In this case, although it can be unclear where an employers responsibilities lie (Kaupins and Park 2011), the employer took the position that they were legally responsible for online harassment via SNSs. However, in this instance, and indeed, some of the others above we see how employers, rather than dealing with an issue that could be associated with SNSs by interrogating it, take very simplistic action via attempts at banning access. As I have mentioned in the case of the school, however, and as I shall expand in more detail later, clearly a greater number of employees have access to smartphones and are circumventing policies and technical blocks using these devices. However, it is not just personal devices that are being enrolled, in order to mirror some of the social aspects that SNSs afford for colleagues – some employees find ways of appropriating organisational arrangements. Here, Aleksy talked of using the employer's network messaging system to socialise with colleagues in addition to using it for conducting work. A scene from the film *Jumping Jack Flash* is pertinent here in pointing to narratives regarding such practice. In this fictional scene, the character Terry Doolittle (played by Whoopi Goldberg) is chastised by her boss for using the bank's international transfer system to share recipes for Yankee Pot Roast and to provide sex advice to a bank worker in France – Jean Claude. This film, released in 1986, pre-dates the mass uptake of the Internet and SNSs, and although fictional, provides a historical reference point regarding employee appropriation of organisational arrangements to engage in personal sociality.

One final point to make in this section is that employers may also lead employees to engage in disconnective practice because they have attempted to connect with them in ways that the employee feels is inappropriate. Aleksy discussed such a case in his interview telling the story of how his employer tried to contact an employee, via Facebook, whilst he was on holiday in order to resolve an organisational problem. As a result of the contact, the employee deleted their Facebook account so they would not be bothered whilst they were on a break in the future. Consequently not only might employers be responsible for employees disconnecting with SNSs at work, this can bleed into their personal lives as well, and potentially where the role in question is not an issue.

The effects of the nature and structure of work

In this chapter, I have so far referred to the idea that a type of role at work might be implicated in disconnective practices. In this section, I will explore this a little further and go on to explore in greater detail the additional role of the structuring of work. The type of job people engage with might affect the enactment of disconnective practice for some people. Within the group of people in this study, it was those who worked in public service who usually spoke of not engaging with SNSs because of their role. In this respect engaging in disconnective practice was often concerned with a need to protect the public they were working with or on behalf of in some way. For example, teachers spoke of not giving out data regarding their students, and health workers discussed patient confidentiality. That said the nature of work also afforded connectivity for some of the participants. These participants worked in a more independent fashion and engaged in connecting the personal and work. Indeed, there was potential value seen in doing this. For Ela, she saw her personal networks in Facebook as a mode by which she could spread the message regarding a professional blog she wanted to set up on the topic of international cultures. This blog, she said would also be connected with her professional presence on LinkedIn. For Suzanne, her use of Facebook included running a Facebook page that through which she took bookings for her Pet Salon and using her own profile page to display and sell her artworks. Finally, even though Jenny was a school teacher, she was able to create an account in Twitter that used a pseudonym in order to consume personal content and follow other teachers for professional purposes. In this context she said no one knew who she was and so could operate in both roles quite comfortably referring to her followers as "faceless Internet people". A final point to make regarding the nature of work and disconnective practice relates to the relevance of a given SNSs to particular roles. Here I particularly want to single out LinkedIn, as many of the participants of this study did. Simply put, several participants did not connect with LinkedIn as they saw it having no relevance to the work that they did at the time of the interview, it had no value for them:

> Because it would get me no-where. Because with the type of job I've got at the moment or the stuff I want to do is completely useless to me, but I can understand if maybe you ran a business or something, something a bit more high profile, then yes, it might be useful.
>
> (Hannah, sales assistant, 25–34)

> LinkedIn is a professional sort of connection site, for professional people in business, as far as I'm aware. I'm not sure if it's for anything else. So no, I don't really have any, I don't need to network on a professional sense, I don't need contacts and business associates. I know enough train drivers, I know too many train drivers! So, it just doesn't serve a purpose for me.
>
> (Matt, train driver, 35–44)

As Hannah and Matt demonstrate, the value of LinkedIn was seen to be related to professional roles. Although I agree with Wittel (2001) that there is something of a social trickling-down effect from higher management to the "shop floor" of the corporate world, where it comes to the enrolment of networking practices, the extent to which this has extended beyond corporate and professional boundaries is less clear. Employment role can have some influence, for some people, on whether they would choose to connect via a route such as this. For others, like Nina, they also said they would not know anyone within that network were they to join, as their work colleagues and friends were not on

LinkedIn either. The interesting point here is that anyone with access to the appropriate equipment (as people like Hannah, Matt and Nina have) could create an account on LinkedIn if they wanted to. However, clearly the marketing of the LinkedIn network, by the company and its participants, and the infrastructure of the SNS itself is working to exclude and disconnect some people. LinkedIn as an SNS itself can therefore be seen to be complicit in asking people to engage in disconnective practice. To be clear, I am not saying that there are no "non-professionals" operating within LinkedIn – there are. My point is that a particular set of sociotechnical arrangements, inscribed with expectations of job roles, can dissuade connection when it is in fact their job to encourage it. Or to clarify my latter point, and importantly, to encourage it for particular job roles in order for its users to continue to see value in the network.

SNSs use at, or for, work might involve disconnective practice due to the actual structures of the work being performed. These structures might relate to the work itself. Jason spoke of his past employment in a restaurant as waiting staff, where he felt it was not right to be seen to be on your phone in front of customers. Wayne told of how, for the most part of his day, he was at a desk speaking with patients (as an occupational therapist) and therefore it was not appropriate or possible to access SNSs during that time. However, many people did mention breaks in their work that allowed them to access SNSs – this involved coffee or lunch breaks, but also trips to printers, drinks machines or photocopiers too. As Miller (2011) has argued, SNSs can change the relationship between work and leisure and there are minimal options for stopping people carrying on with their personal lives in the workplace. Disconnective practice might also relate to the physical environment and infrastructure at work. Here, for instance, Bob (a cleaner) said that obviously he did not have access to a computer for his job (though he did access SNSs on his phone for personal purposes) and it was a similar situation for Matt (a train driver). Moreover, Jenny discussed the problem with the weak 3G connection at school which meant she had difficulties connecting, even in breaks and Hannah told of how everyone can see her computer screen at work and so she did not access SNSs there just in case what she called "a crazy picture or something" appeared. However, the layout of a work environment was also seen as something that allowed for connection and physical disconnective practice.

> I work at my parents' takeaway at weekend and I use Facebook while I work, under the counter.
>
> (Xui Li, student, 16–24)

Like messaging behind the scenes in Facebook or LinkedIn or using the backchannel of Facebook, the counter in Xui Li's parents' takeaway afforded her the ability to connect without the public seeing her activity. This was not dissimilar to Ian's story of staff at the school he worked at using mobiles in the staff room, at a school that had a zero tolerance policy for students viz the use of such devices.

Yet, despite the possibilities for engaging with SNSs at work, within the structures of work they were bound with, the participants discussed how they would only do this under certain conditions because they did not want it to interfere with them doing their job. For example, Hannah reported using SNSs to listen to music as she worked, but stated that watching video would be problematic, and Kevin and Nina said they would send a few messages via Facebook if they had time but would not browse the site as that would be too distracting. Only one person, who happened to be unhappy in their role at work, said they would engage with SNSs to an extent that it stopped them from doing their job. SNSs share commonalities with many of the technologies that are developed for business purposes in that they too are useful for social purposes (and vice versa). These prior technologies have been argued to have, much to irritation of employers, decreased rather than increased worker productivity whilst at the same time increasing their socialising at work (Rice and Love 1987, Schmitz and Fulk 1991). However, the participants in the study paint a complex picture as to the extent to which SNSs emulate the appropriation of previous technological arrangements intended for work. It is not necessarily the case that SNSs will have a detrimental impact upon an organisational performance though. As the participants of this study demonstrate, a high degree of self regulation is engaged at work, as necessary.

Conclusion

Clearly the connective affordances of SNSs offer continuities in respect of our understandings of the boundary between the personal, or home, and work. A greater number of people are now engaging with SNSs, and for many these activities are becoming intertwined with their employment status, irrespective of what their occupation or employment status is. Such connections may be planned, accidental, enacted under pressure from others or indeed by others. That said, disconnective practice is still an important feature of this area of SNS appropriation. Disconnective practice features in basic questions of whether to link work and the personal by choosing who, related to work, will and will not be connected with via SNSs. It is also evident in decisions regarding whether or not SNSs accounts that are classified as work or personal are linked. Moreover, my participants reported engaging in the retro-editing of activity as disconnective practice as a way of refining their presentation of self into something that they felt would be palatable to current and future employers and colleagues. Beyond attempts to carve out identities and spaces with SNSs that suited contemporary employment contexts, once they were in place (in as much as they could be), disconnective practices were enrolled in relation to whether work was talked about in these or not. Such strategies employed blanket approaches of not discussing work at all through to more nuanced attempts at providing cover to allow for work discussion to take place. Additionally we see here how employers may instruct employees to engage in disconnective practice by specifying policies which preclude the discussion of work via SNSs. Organisational policies were also used to mandate employee disconnection at work in a number of ways and more practical approaches of technological barrier creation were common. The final area of disconnection I discuss is the roles of the nature and structure of an individual's occupation, where we see for instance notions of time, layout of work space, customer and service-user engagement, and importantly the perceived relevance of networking to someone's role all playing a part in shaping the potential for appropriation.

In summary, what I hope I have added to the discussion regarding SNSs and work is the need to take seriously the diversity of people's work experiences in relation to discourses regarding the benefits and problems and SNSs in the domain. Moreover, not only does this diversity affect how people use SNSs, it also colours how they might shy away from use or only partially engage in use. Indeed, such usage possibilities might not rest with the user in question; others may dictate access, even where use is required. Indeed, the condition where use is not perceived to be necessary is particularly interesting. Perhaps the most insidious form of disconnective practice is that which convinces those outside of the professions, creative industries and digerati, that digital networking is not for them and therefore those people lose out on any potential benefits.

However, I believe there is hope for change here and I would like to end this chapter with a short note on this. My ethnographic work on Facebook, identified many people engaging with it in order to network, for formal work purposes. Although Facebook is not instantly thought of as an employment-networking environment of course it is used as such, and it is not just restricted to the professions, creative and the digerati.

One example that stands out particularly is a woman who runs much of her Ann Summers business through Facebook. Ann Summers is a British-based retailer that specialises in selling sex toys and lingerie. It is clear through my connection with this woman that she is a team leader and runs competitions for her team through the network in order to increase sales. She also uses the network to promote parties at which products are sold, seek volunteers to host parties, post news about discounts and sales, and even to recruit women to her team. The team in question is also active in engaging with each other in terms of promoting each other's activities, parties and also in respect of sharing experiences and tips. This group of women have appropriated Facebook to support them in a number of traditional organisational functions such as HR, sales, marketing and, of course, networking. What makes this example even more interesting is that Ann Summers' products are sexually charged and these women deftly navigate the terms and conditions of Facebook, with respect to sexual content, with ease via the use of linguistic cover or redactional acumen. Therefore, while I have suggested that sites such as LinkedIn might engage in disconnective practice, rule out certain people participating; and consequently that they may loose out on the value such arrangements might be said to provide, at the same time some are crafting their own business networks in other spaces.

Part III
Personal Disconnection

6
Personalising Use

Introduction

I agree with Stewart (2007) who argues that as we, as individuals, become more engaged with information and communications technologies, it is important to understand the heterogeneous sets of relationships that are brought into play. In this chapter of the book I want to focus upon how we personalise the use of SNSs by engaging with disconnective practice. Of course, connection is clearly important here too, and has been for sometime where the Internet is concerned more generally (Licklider and Taylor 1968, Kennedy and Wellman 2007). More specifically as related to SNSs, the importance of connection is made evident by much prior work whether this, for instance, is concerned with how our prior and current interests might affect our desires to connect with SNSs (Baym and Ledbetter 2009, Hargittai and Litt 2011, Hargittai and Litt 2012); friending practices (boyd 2006, Richardson and Hessey 2009); approaches to privacy (Gross and Acquisti 2005, Patchin and Hinduja 2010); the development of social capital (Joinson 2008) and even connection just for connection's sake (Miller 2008). Moreover, as I have already shown, it is a key feature of the work I present here. Indeed, as Nina recounted regarding her experience of personal use:

> It is positive to have your Spotify account linked to your Facebook account because other people make really good playlists and then you can listen to their playlist
>
> (Nina, sales assistant, 16–24)

and as Daphne elaborated:

> ...my grandchildren do follow me on Twitter. It was when they, one of the grandchildren said "it's sad when your grandmother has more followers than you". I still have [laughs].
>
> (Daphne, local councillor, 65+)

People are connecting and attempting to connect, in personal situations, via SNSs. An array of connection techniques were mentioned during the interviews, including the use of liking, following, sharing, hash tagging, photo tagging, status updating, adding, tweeting, among others. Yet, we also know connection can bring problems. As has been reported widely in SNS research and the popular press, I also found that such problems are wide ranging. This study included such problems as that of the somewhat comical story of Xui Li's father's obsession with SNS-mediated gaming where he called her at 2am asking her for more lives as he had exhausted his own, and his wife's, lives on their Candy Crush Facebook accounts, and to the potentially relationship damaging impact of a television appearance combined with Twitter (See Table 6.1).

Table 6.1 A story of unrequited following

I don't know if this counts as me having a problem, but I remember when my other half, he did this TV thing and he got loads of women following him on Twitter and I hated it. I knew it wasn't his fault...it wasn't like Facebook where you make friends and if they tried to add him as a friend he wouldn't have let them. On Twitter they can just follow you and you don't have a say in it really. And he didn't follow them back and he didn't do anything wrong...but I hated it. I hated that. So that did cause a problem, I was quite upset about that, even though it was maybe irrational and ridiculous, but I think that's the only problem really. But things like that can cause...can cause issues. I remember when that happened I kind of Googled it: "Am I being irrational to be upset about this?" and somebody had put on there that she was 25 and her boyfriend had lots of friends who were single girls around their age, she didn't like that because he'd met them online it made her uncomfortable...I actually discussed it a lot with him at the time saying this is potentially new problems in relationships. After he'd been on TV and he'd got these women following him, who'd actually proposed "Oh, I'm in love with him, marry me" and things like that...[It was]...because the program featured on Twitter. There was a Twitter feed about it, and people from his work were tagging the programme and tagging his Twitter handle so that everybody could then see what his Twitter handle was. So he hadn't done it, and I was getting annoyed with everyone at work for doing that, but they were doing it innocently, but he'd got loads of people following him because they had tagged both the Twitter handle and the programme, so then that gave everybody who was looking at the hash tag for the programme, his...so they started following him. And actually, they still follow him. He could block them, and he would if I asked him to, but actually I've got over it now, really. Just at the time I didn't like it. But they're still there. Nothing's come of it or anything.

Rebecca, school teacher, 35–44.

For me the question is one of how we conceptualise the ways people are dealing with the sometimes-overwhelming push for connectivity that has pervaded our contemporary existence. In this chapter I will consider some themes that will add further colour to the idea of disconnective practice. These themes include: attention to how disconnection is present in the navigation of relationships, identity work, our editorial ethics, the exercise of agency in relation to SNS features, and the structural effects of SNS features we may wrestle with.

Navigating personal relationships

Disconnection featured in a number of ways in the area of personal relationships. Katie for example, told of how within a circle of friends one person did not use Instagram and that led to issues when everyone met up to eat at each other's houses or a restaurant. Whilst all but one person busily Instagrammed their food, Katie noted that the person who did not use that SNS was left out of the activity. In effect, Instagram facilitated disconnection amongst the group. Disconnection was also present in other mundane aspects of personal relationships – gossiping via SNSs was also talked about by several interview participants. As the following example given by Simon shows this involves disconnective practice in the sense of using things, such as private messaging facilities or backchannels, to create places for activity to take place:

> I think the only things that I've had is the circle of friends that I met through Gaydar, that I then became friends with on Facebook, there's been quite a bit of bitching and backstabbing going on through Facebook within that circle of people. It's not been caused by the social networking sites, they've just been a vessel to assist with it because we all know each other in person, we go out for nights out, it's the fact that you've got Facebook there as a vessel for two people to whisper about somebody else behind their back. It still happens in person when you're out on a night out, but you've got that added thing on Facebook where you can private message someone and you can talk about someone behind their back.
>
> (Simon, civil servant, 25–34)

Beyond the practice of engaging with people you know via SNSs, participants also talked about how they might disconnect with people in a variety of ways. Although it has been argued that "by tying Friendship to privacy settings, social network sites encourage people to choose Friends based on what they want to make visible" (boyd 2006: sic), extra work is undertaken to allow for friending and for relationships to develop within this kind of environment. A common mode of practice here was the hiding of posts by certain people if they were seen as offensive or undesirable in some way. A key reason for this was that it allowed people to avoid what they saw as a potentially awkward situation, where they had to explain to someone why they had unfriended or unfollowed them. As Andy explained:

> I've unsubscribed a few people. I'd never speak to them in real life and say "why are you posting that shit" and everything, it's their choice, they can do what they want but its affected the fact that, yes I would ignore, but it doesn't affect your real life because again, it's in their own time, if they want to post all that stuff then they can. It doesn't affect me as I just don't see it anymore. And if they wanted to contact me, they would never do it via their wall function; they would send me a message so I don't think that they know that I'm ignoring them.
>
> (Andy, legal professional, 25–34)

Other reasons for hiding people were due to them being seen as boring, as posting irrelevant content – or too much content. As Rebecca recalled, "you don't want to see 85 posts a day about kittens". Here again though, the larger point is that by taking such action, a form of relationship could be maintained within the space. However, despite people acknowledging the removal of friends, or "friend culling" as something not to be done lightly, this was also a widespread practice. This was done to help people make better sense of the content being shared within their networks – so they could focus on the people who were deemed to matter. Those being culled were usually people who participants had previously worked with or people they had lost touch with rather than what were described as close personal friends. Further in order to mitigate against the need for future friend culls, further disconnective practices were enrolled. For example, Jason spoke of how he did no longer accepted friend requests from people he worked with and Ela outlined how she held some friend requests in abeyance whilst she decided if it was going to be worth enrolling them in her network:

> I suppose in terms of Facebook I usually don't connect with people who I don't know. For instance my boyfriend's friends who have heard of me but I've never met them or maybe I have had a brief hello with them, and they send me invitations on Facebook and I feel really

rude not to accept them but I don't accept them because I don't know them. And I leave it, I don't decline it, I leave it hanging and if I get an opportunity to meet them, I would, but other than that, no.

(Ela, translator, 25–34)

Ela adopted a very similar strategy when it came to non-human invitations to connect. She explained how her friends told her she must try out a new Facebook game, and so after much pressure, she did. However, when asked by the game if she wanted to connect her account, she declined. She said this was because she wanted to try the game out first without it being networked – just to see if she liked it. She tried the game out and decided to delete it from her phone without ever establishing the connectivity it.

Identity work

Identity work is a strong feature of SNS research, for instance in terms of the roles of group and individual interactions (boyd 2006, Light et al. 2008) and our abilities to craft expression of tastes and preferences (Light 2007, Liu 2007b, Baym and Ledbetter 2009, Davis 2010). Again it is possible here to see how disconnection can play a role. For example, the deployment of strategies to maintain anonymity within such sites, even where the real name Web is concerned can involve disconnective practice. Katie, for instance, discussed how the anonymity of identity was made possible in Flickr and how the perceived lack of such a possibility for anonymity in Facebook fractured a community:

we were really active for about 2 or 3 years[on Flickr] and then Facebook started. And that's when it got tricky because with Flickr we were able to be as anonymous as we wanted, so for instance, one of my best friends on Flickr is a Red Massey Ferguson Tractor, that's his icon, and he's got pseudonym and obviously we got to know each other through words so it didn't matter that we didn't know what he looked like or what his name was. But then when Facebook started, that's because of friend of a friend architecture, that made it very difficult for people to remain anonymous and so some of the groups didn't join Facebook. And all of a sudden Facebook made people make their friending choices explicit and basically within 6 months, our community had imploded, there were several fallouts.

(Katie, social technologist, 35–44)

The desire for anonymity of identity was also talked about in terms of why people might not choose to connect accounts. Nina spoke of how she was able to share much more personal information via her Tumblr account than with Facebook or Twitter because she used a pseudonym. Moreover, she explained that because of this she would not connect her Tumblr accounts with Twitter or Facebook where she shared different kinds of information with others about herself. In effect she wanted to reveal different aspects of herself in different places and engaged in disconnective practice to allow for this.

Nina's approach of presenting different versions of herself was also mentioned by other participants. Simon and Bob both created multiple accounts within Facebook to distinguish between accounts which they saw were for the "mundane aspects" of their daily lives, such as catching up with friends, and the identities they created for performance purposes. Simon has an account for his alter ego, Paula. Paula is a larger than life trans character who visits at a variety of LGBT bars and clubs in northern England. Bob created a Facebook page for his band. Therefore, it is important to place a reminder here that disconnective practice is not necessarily about resistance or navigating problems associated with SNSs, it is something that adds value to people's experiences and allows them to operate as they want to with such spaces. Yet, like technologies which pre-date SNSs, such as email, we see parallels. Crafting messages for multiple recipients is complex, requiring attendance to a diversity of audience (Skovholt and Svennevig 2006). To borrow the thinking of Dena (2008), one might then think of disconnective practice as involving "tiering". Tiering refers to the material points of entry of, in Dena's terms, a world or work. This tiering involves providing access to separate content to different audiences. Such a provision of content involves, I would argue, connection and disconnection, sometimes simultaneously. This point is further reinforced by Simon's usage of both his and Paula's accounts in tandem to generate further interest in his alter ego – he often connects the two by creating dialogue between them:

> They're just down as friends, they will, because the alter ego profile is very much a character profile, and because of the way that I've always portrayed the character within that profile, there's occasions when the two of us will have an argument via status. But that's the only connection we have with those.
>
> (Simon, civil servant, 25–34)

Simon and Bob's experiences also remind us that identity work is about creating ourselves through our actions. This was a further reason for people engaging in disconnective practice in this area – because they used different sites for different purposes, and those purposes were not seen as relevant parts of their lives for everyone that they knew. For example:

- Ela wanted to keep her personal activities on Facebook separate from her work based activities on LinkedIn;
- Kevin separated his tweeting about non-conventional versions of history and conspiracy theories apart from his friends on Facebook;
- Jenny kept her interests in teaching practice, followed on Twitter, separate from her Facebook activity which was described as for people she knew in "real life";
- Jyoti's LinkedIn networking was detached from her attendance at music festivals.

Part of the desire for interview participants to disconnect aspects of themselves was revealed to be concerned with not wanting to be judged for certain activities they engaged with. Nina, for instance, did not want her friends knowing she was listening to "cheesy" music, so she often created private sessions on Spotify so it did not transmit details of this to her Facebook friends. She also mentioned using the application, Side Reel, in the same way saying that "I don't want to link it because I watch quite a lot of very bad TV and I don't want everyone to see that I constantly watch The Only Way is Essex". Ela also told a similar story in relation to SNS-linked games:

> And it almost feels like a bit of a shame factor when if it constantly posts on your Facebook that you crashed this level on whatever game, it feels like you've nothing else in your life but to play on a game. So I suppose there is a bit of that that you don't really want people to see it.
>
> (Ela, translator, 25–34)

Ela and Nina were aware of general discourses regarding SNSs and the values placed upon particular media and therefore, engaged in disconnective practice to allow them to enjoy this without facing embarrassment or judgment. Such judgement regarding media, particularly the playing of SNS-based games did emerge in the interviews. For example, when asked about how people felt about those who played SNS games, Hannah said she might "judge them a little bit", Sarah referred to them as "daft games" and Jason said he hated the requests he got from people for things like Bejewelled and Farmville. Notably, Ela, Nina, Hanna, Sarah and Jason are all in the category of what has been described as the Gamer Generation – those youth almost hard-wired with particular preferences and abilities as a result of growing up with digital games (Beck and Wade 2006), illustrating of course the overly simplistic nature of such all encompassing labels. It is also interesting to compare this state of affairs with the work of Holin and Chuen-Tsai (2011). Holin and Chuen-Tsai's study of gamer audiences that richly demonstrates how onlookers become integral to gameplay in public videogame arcades, acting as engaged audience, focused apprentice and uninterested person next in line. Where connection dominates in their work, aside possibly, from the small number of those uninterested persons waiting in line for their turn, the connective attempts of Facebook games translate into disconnection. This is because unlike Holin and Cheun-Tsai's participants, one might say "the arcade" was forced upon the participants in the study. My participant's experiences are perhaps likened to having to walk past a serious of loud arcades along the front of a UK seaside town when all one wants to do is get to the other end to meet a friend for coffee and cake. A further strategy deployed to avoid judgement and embarrassment via disconnective practice was the enrolment of safe spaces:

> I'd try it out on Facebook first and if I got enough likes I'd put it on Twitter. No, even though I'm joking, I would test the water before letting people I might know see it. I know that makes me sound incredibly shallow.
>
> (Andy, legal professional, 25–34)

Here Andy reported using Facebook as a separate test bed for ideas and would then only share these further if he felt the audience reaction there made them worthy of posting via his Twitter account – which he saw as more important. In addition to attempting to avoid judgment or embarrassment, Andy's strategy was also one of optimising his contributions to SNSs for maximum success and impact through compartmentalised disconnective practice enabled experimentation.

Editorial ethics

Disconnective practice is clearly at work in the editing of what we share with SNSs – we live a process of deciding what to include, or not, and also engaging with others in what we share about them, and vice versa. We create contexts to contextualise our performances for those we imagine or intend to be our audience within SNSs (boyd 2011). This involves us making decisions about the extent to which we post and share and the nature of what we post and share. This was a theme that was visited time and again in the interviews and of course it is here, in different ways in this chapter, and throughout the rest of the book. Here however, I wanted to discuss the enrolment of disconnective practice in editorial ethics, a term familiar to journalism. By using the term editorial ethics here, I refer to the idea that the editing of our SNS practice can be influenced by what we and others see as a morally right action. It can involve action we take and actions others take in the publishing process. Importantly, this is a disconnective practice that not only seeks to do what is deemed to be the right thing by others, but the right thing by ourselves too. Such a position is grounded in prior work which has demonstrated the material importance of ethics in digitally mediated spaces and in relation to digital media (Nissenbaum 1995, Johnson 1997, Johnson 2001, Adam 2005, Craft 2007, Introna 2007, Wolfendale 2007, Ess 2009) and more specifically SNSs (Griffiths and Light 2008, Light and McGrath 2010). Such an editorial ethics may involve self-censorship and perhaps here the most obvious example would be those people who do not post about work. As Jenny stated: "I think I'm pretty sensible so I'd never post anything defamatory or that could jeopardise my job." But such practice is broader in terms of people not wanting to cause harm for themselves. In the quote below we see how Julie talks of a desire, and attempts, to avoid multiple harms across different situations:

> When I was off sick after my partner died I used it [Facebook] as a link to people and a bit of fun. I'm sat here every night on my own, so it was just a bit of a way to socialise, but not leave the house. [I was] careful not to put anything that even slightly make me happy because I was off [work] with depression and bereavement, so I daren't even put anything happy or positive on, but then I don't like putting all miserable stuff on. Yeah. My friend had taken me shopping and, in Asda, she takes stupid photographs of me in Asda. She found a packet of cock-flavoured soup; it has a picture of a cockerel on the front, which she made a post with it. So I'm like that, with

this cock-flavoured soup. So she posted it on Facebook and I'm like "But I'm supposed to be off sick with depression!" So I were waiting for the backlash off that, but no one ever said anything.

(Julie, health care assistant, 35–44)

Julie's experience also points to SNS users often needing to negotiate with other people regarding the potential for the creation of harm and their ethical positions regarding this. Andy also described a situation where this negotiation had to take place:

...like I say now you can moderate when people tag you in places and stuff like that. So I can do that. When I was out a few weeks ago, and I really shouldn't have been out because I was quite skint, but I went out and met up with some friends and I said "I'm at my parents tomorrow and my sister will be there and if you tag me, she'll see", and they were like "oh you have to approve it don't you", and I was like "yes, but because she's friends with all of you, she's going to see it anyway, whether I'm tagged or not, she'll see it on your pages".

(Andy, legal professional, 25–34)

Moreover, people will also engage in disconnective practice to protect people they are connected with; this was often talked about in terms of a duty of care. From a different perspective, but similar to Andy's experience, Ela told of how "if you are with someone that should be working and they've pulled a sickie or something like that, you wouldn't tag them because you don't know who can see that", and Rebecca told of how she had to advise another family member to remove a post related to her father:

David's sister-in-law put on once on Facebook... "Thanks for the free bus ride" and I'd emailed straight away and said "Take that off", because if somebody from his work sees that he could lose his job for letting people on for free. So...I even, kind of warned other people about it because I didn't want there to be any repercussions for her doing that. So I'm very aware of it, because it, you know, people get in trouble. Yeah.

(Rebecca, school teacher, 35–44)

The problems that the persistence of information available within networked publics caused was commonly tacitly, if not explicitly acknowledged. Furthermore, we see how such practices emulate those of prior arrangements such as email where the "copying in" of recipients, as a form of tagging, invited participation beyond the primary addressee (Skovholt and Svennevig 2006). Indeed, this practice of copying pre-dates email, as Skovholt and Svennevig elaborate, the copying of letters preceded this.

A final dimension that was raised during interviews was the extent to which people thought of others as related to their sharing practices. A recurring theme here that it was "not right" to "clog up" people's newsfeeds with unnecessary stories or updates from apps, games or themselves. For instance, Andy, Ela and Matt mentioned not wanting to be the person who constantly posted in people's newsfeeds about their gaming activities, and Aleksey said he limited himself to two to three posts a day and Nina talked of the need not to share things that had already been shared within her network. Therefore, disconnective practice in this way operates as a mode by which respect for others can be exercised. However, Tom also told of how experiencing a lack of restraint by others caused him harm and led him to not engage with shared SNS content unless he trusted the person it originated from. Tom spoke of watching a YouTube video within Facebook that featured a person being beheaded. He said it caused him distress and that there was no warning beforehand. As Hargittai et al. (2012) state, it may be some time before the norms of appropriate use and skills at filtering within SNSs start to stabilise.

Exercising agency in relation to SNS features

Perhaps one of the most pervasive modes of disconnective practice, and indeed SNS use is that of lurking, whether that is using SNSs to follow celebrities (Marwick and boyd 2011a, Murphy 2013) or to engage in participatory surveillance where we contribute to the building of subjectivities through information sharing whilst at the same time observing others (Albrechtslund 2012). Everyone in the study practiced this form of dis/engagement. In doing so, users generally rebuff the connective advances of SNSs. However, it is important to remember that within some sites, such as YouTube, where users have accounts, the history of viewing/listening practices can be observed if the settings are not adjusted accordingly leaving opportunities for connections to be established. Indeed of course, connections can also be established without such features in place, for instance where a discussion about someone's latest status update, tweet or photo upload is discussed over coffee.

That said, lurking remains popular amongst SNS users of varying types, including those without accounts who browse sites such as YouTube and those who observe the activity of other users within spaces that require accounts for access – that is secondary users and bystanders (Ferneley and Light 2006, Ferneley and Light 2008).

Where people have accounts, a further set of practices related to the provision of personal details in profile pages. This was mentioned by several people in relation to concerns as to what might happen if their account was compromised and how this might impact on their financial arrangements, given that many SNSs were perceived to ask for similar details to the security questions ask by financial institutions, such as banks (age and mothers maiden name for instance). For example, Xui Li explained how even her father was aware of such issues:

> My dad's really scared of Facebook. All the private information, he's got the wrong birthday on Facebook; he's 10 years younger as well. Not even the right birthday date. I remember making this thing for him and was like right OK... age dad? Date of birth 1st January... NO DON'T PUT that, 2nd of February!! I[I said] All this false information, do you want your name on it, or someone else's?? [Laughs] it's funny.
>
> (Xui Li, student, 16–24)

Accordingly here, disconnective practice featured not providing information if it was possible to create an account without it, or by providing false or partially altered information where data was required to proceed. This was not a one-time activity though, that would necessarily happen at account set up, and when this was strategy was engaged retrospectively, for Kevin it created problems with his partner:

> I did something which a lot of people do which is I deleted my personal information off Facebook and I didn't realise but what that then does is it comes up and says "you are no longer in a relationship with somebody" which didn't go down very well, but I just didn't want any personal information on my Facebook page anymore, I want it to just be plain, I didn't want it to say all those things about what you like and where you are, all that kind of stuff.
>
> (Kevin, sales assistant, 25–34)

The modes of not providing information extended to the engagement of functions of particular sites too. Several participants reported not using functions aimed at, amongst other things, the distribution of information throughout their networks, including those related to liking, sharing, retweeting and tagging. It might also involve not using such features, as discussed earlier, and instead rejecting (to an extent) automated data collection via the cutting and pasting of URLs rather than using share features as discussed in earlier chapters. Moreover, where such actions were taken by others, and which included them when it wasn't desirable, additional disconnective practices where brought to bear whereby, for example, people did not accept for things to be placed within their timeline on Facebook or they removed tags from particular posts or photographs. Such activity might also extend to involving others. Disconnective practice can be something that you ask others to engage in on your behalf as Jyoti explained:

> The only thing I've ever had as a...I got married and somebody put photos of...the wedding photos all on Facebook before we'd even had a chance to look at the photos, and I did ask Rafi's sister and a friend of mine. I asked them to remove the photos as soon as I saw them because I didn't feel particularly comfortable with that. I mean, they took them down straight away but I found that quite a weird use of Facebook. It's fine...yeah, weird. Because we hadn't put any photos on but they had already gone ahead and done that. So that's the only issue I've ever had with it really.
>
> (Jyoti, sales director, 35–44)

A final example relating to the exercise of agency with SNS features is that where users aim to not be contactable via SNSs. Of course, this can be achieved via not logging into SNSs, but in order to lurk, some SNSs require users to do this. Logging on of course does not necessarily mean you will be contactable; however, as Andy mentioned in Chapter 3, certain sites can signal you are logged in (a registering of a read mail in Facebook for example, or a retweet in Twitter) and this can prompt others to attempt to connect with you. However, it became clear in the interviews that whilst participants wanted to enter SNSs, they often did so for a particular purpose and their intention was not to connect with everyone in their network, as Julie explains:

> On Facebook, you know, you can show that you're online and I don't, no. But it were for the reason of, if you show them online you get loads of people private messaging and...you know, you can do instant chat? And get loads of people wanting to talk to you, and

I just can't be bothered. So no one knows that I'm on unless I've just said something or liked something, then it will say just things like this. So yeah, I don't show that I'm on it.

(Julie, health care assistant, 35–44)

Disconnective practice might then involve adjusting settings to reduce the possibility for synchronous communication attempts. This adds to our understanding of how disconnective practice facilitates the management of asynchronous communication attempts, as discussed in Chapter 3.

Case study: Exercising disconnective agency in Habbo hotel

Habbo is a three-dimensional social networking space aimed at 13–18 year olds. Users have a profile and an avatar – a Habbo. Habbos are used to play and network throughout public and private rooms which are dedicated to a range of activities. Members can decorate their private rooms with virtual furniture or "furni" which is bought with Habbo credits. Habbo credits are purchased using currency from the physical world and consequently have material economic value. Apart from a wide range of standard furni available, to buy or trade, rare furni, prizes or seasonal furni can also be bought or won by participating in online games. Other revenue is generated by in-world advertising. The Habbos are heavily targeted by organisations such as Coca-Cola, Nike, EMI, Gillette, Procter and Gamble, and PlayStation. This marketing extends to "live" celebrity appearances, where Habbos can engage in conversation with their favourite film star or watch a "live music" concert.

Habbo can be classified in different ways and this, can lead to different ethical takes on the space. Here though, I wish to draw on my previous work, led by Marie Griffiths (Griffiths and Light 2008), to explore how disconnective practice might be engaged with in order to challenge the philosophy of an SNS and obtain economic benefit. More specifically, I am interested in scammers who operate within Habbo. In effect some members engage in a range of scamming practices in order to dupe other members into providing access to their furni (see Table 6.2). This furni has material economic value and can be sold, unofficially, through channels such as eBay, often at a significant price where rare furni items are concerned. The scamming activity undertaken within Habbo is decidedly against the philosophy of the site and Sulake, the company behind Habbo, make clear that this is the case in their terms and conditions of service. However, scammers choose to disconnect with this philosophy

Table 6.2 Scamming games in Habbo

Email scamming	Scammers send email designed to mimic official Habbo e-mail. The email directs members to bogus login pages and there details are stolen.
Furni cloning	Habbos claim that they can clone furni by placing it in a certain place or by clicking the mouse a number of times. They obtain member account details to do this and then steal their furni.
Gold digging	Scammers pose as being interested in being someone's partner or get married to someone in order to gain favour and access to their account.
Rogue decorators	Habbos pose as decorators, offer to decorate a room and obtain member account details to do this. The room is cleared of furni by the scammers.
Prostitution	Scammers pose as "furni whores" who offer to perform cybersex in return for furni. Furni is handed over, but the cybersex does not happen.

Adapted from Griffiths and Light (2008).

and indeed the more general ethos of connectivity for sociality in order to make money. To be clear, scammers are not interested in connection and sociality; however, they are interested in connectivity and socialisation. Socialisation is a key function of the connection required during scamming as shown in Table 6.2.

It is not just the philosophy of the site that the scammers choose to disconnect with. In order to justify their ethics, the scammers interviewed were quick to point out that Habbo was not a real space. As one scammer put it:

Deceiving people? We are probably chatting to a 40-year-old guy who is pretending to be some kid. Let's get real no one is who they say they are, no-one. You have to have a totally different mentality on-line, totally different. It is not how we act IRL. We are not robbing off old ladies, you can't get arrested for it, it is totally different – the only thing they can do is block your account or IP address. Would I steal in IRL? No it is totally different, yeah, yeah, yeah, some Dutch kid got arrested but that is 1 in a million, it is the chance you take of getting your account banned, that is the fun, beating Habbo.

The narrative detailed above was a common one amongst scammers and our analysis suggested that our participants were having difficulty making connections between their activity in Habbo and that in other spaces because they did not see Habbo as real. Habbo was seen as a space of fantasy and play. The gaming elements of Habbo overshadowed the SNS elements and the scammers saw themselves as merely making another game up in a gaming space. These scamming practices occurred even despite the signifiers of the physical world, such as live performances and advertising, being present with it. Therefore in this case, disconnective practice was enrolled to create distance from reality in order to allow for behaviours to play out that would not in physical space. Depending upon one's stance, such behaviours might be seen as both ethically questionable and economically valuable. Moreover, it is important to point out how the philosophy of connection associated with SNSs is also central to this practice. The scamming could not occur if other Habbos did not choose to connect with the scammers nor if the mediators associated with Habbo such as private rooms, furni and communication arrangements were not in place.

Structural effects of SNS features

I am trying to demonstrate throughout this book, the constant mutual shaping of us and the SNSs we engage with. In the previous two sections, I emphasised human agency in this respect and in this section I want to emphasise the role of SNSs as structures which aim to determine our actions. One might say that a key ingredient of SNSs is their ability to keep connection in place, working and not stagnant. If we follow this line of argument, then a question arises as to how many requests to participate can we manage? Aside from a few participants, such as Denise and Katie, self-confessed mediaphiles, many found the ability to main multiple accounts a struggle, because the structures of them required too much effort to have them work properly as they saw it. Aleksy's comment of "I personally felt I was wasting too much time" and Julie's "not another one" – were emblematic of such discourses. This discourse also extended to the adoption of the features of in SNS apps, such as games. Despite the game's structures being inscribed with connectivity that attempted to shape gameplay, this did not always play out:

> some of the games I used to play on Facebook, yes. But I tend not to, I can't keep up to them and so I tend to play non-connected games because that way it doesn't matter if I don't go on for a week or two. Whereas, if you playing some that are connected there's all these people who are wanting you to do things and you can do it if you've got the time but if you haven't got the time what's the point? I played

that "city-something", I used to love playing it, but you had to be asking people for things and so on and it could be a month before I got back on again.

(Daphne, local councillor, 65+)

Another feature that shaped interaction was the availability of easy routes to recognition such as the like button in Facebook and the retweet in Twitter. Whilst the sites arguably offer these structural elements to facilitate connectivity, my participants suggested that they sometimes actually led them to disconnect with others. While likes and retweets were seen as easy ways of "social grooming" (Donath 2007b), the problem arose when users were presented with situations where they wanted to quickly demonstrate agreement or disagreement with a post.

I don't like the fact that there isn't an unlike button, or a dislike. Because, well, in some instances people come on to Facebook and, I'm not one of them, and they like "Ooooh no, my brother's died", and you can't like that, can you? I know you're supposed to like it as a thing, but why there isn't a dislike. But I suppose it'd be tantamount to bullying because everybody would just starting disliking certain people's things, you know, like an online bullying forum itself. I can see the reasoning.

(Matt, train driver, 35–44)

To expand on Matt's point further, users wanted an easy way to express negative responses or modes of sentiment that went beyond a "positive" like function. The thumbs-up "like" button, which has been argued to create less a relationship and more of an affective association, requiring less effort (Lovnik 2011), arguably does not offer the range of affective functions users desire, or indeed allow affective processing (Gehl 2011) either. Similarly, within Twitter, it may be easy to retweet a message rather than construct one in response to something. Of course, a retweet could be carrying a message of support, for example, for someone whose brother has just died. However, the participants reported cases where tweets would appear in their feed that either had to be ignored or responded to beyond a retweet because a mere retweet might not generate the right affective association if any at all. Consequently, the structural features of SNSs end up shaping users interactions into forms of disconnective practice because they do not necessarily offer the modes of easy connection users' desire.

The final point I want to make in this section is related to how the structural elements of SNSs might actually disconnect a user without, necessarily, their desire for this to happen. This appears to be counterintuitive to the point I make above regarding the centrality of connection to SNSs. However, it is congruent with the overall argument of this book that connection and disconnection co-exist and are mutually necessary within SNSs. As connection is so important in SNSs, one could argue that structural elements are put in place in an attempt to ensure a quality of connection. This is shown in the work of (Papacharissi 2009), particularly in terms of how the exclusive SNSs ASmallWorld operates. However, such structural elements can also engage in disconnective practice.

> I do know of a certain friend who got banned for...a certain amount of days because he was requesting too many people's friends, to be his friend at a certain time. I don't know why but they give you a limit on how many friend requests you can send, but he was asking all these people and they banned him and stopped him for a certain amount of days and he wasn't happy at all.
>
> (Bob, cleaner, 25–34)

Here Bob is referring to his friend encountering Facebook's rules regarding the amount of friending you can engage in at any one time. Some details of this are given in the extract from Facebook's help pages (Table 6.3). This can be the case with networked apps too. Bob also told of how he could not connect to certain games as you needed at least two friends also playing the game to do so and he only had one.

Table 6.3 Facebook help – friending practice

If your account is temporarily blocked from sending friend requests, it may be because friend requests you've sent have gone unanswered or been marked as unwelcome. In the future, you should send friend requests to people you have a real-life connection to, like your friends, family, co-workers, or classmates. Make sure to use your real name and picture to help the people you're messaging recognise you.

If you're interested in receiving updates from people you find interesting, but don't know personally (e.g. journalists, celebrities, political figures), try following them instead of sending them friend requests.

Facebook 2014.

In its attempt to ensure quality of connection and experience, users can therefore find themselves disconnected from the network.

Dealing with commerce

Our experiences of commerce and the Internet are, to a great extent, rooted in the 1990s where it was envisioned as a space through which one might capture the eyeballs of consumers through this new channel (Schiller 2000). Of course, in addition to this, we saw the development of e-commerce in terms of ideas of the disintermediation of supply chains, the rise of clicks and mortar business and those positioned as being purely online. However if we focus on the contributions of users to the generation of profit for others via the Internet we see this has early beginnings too. Sites such as Yahoo!, AOL and Geocities all relied on users generating content in groups and forums in order to place advertising alongside it in order to generate revenue. The commodification of the private in conjunction with the Internet has also been talked about for some time (Silverstone and Hirsch 1992) and there has been much research which notes, often in Marxist terms, the shift away from value as solely concerned with material production (Lash 2002, Röhle 2007) and its embedding within the most intimate aspects of our lives – such as dating (Fiore and Donath 2004, Arvidsson 2006, Magnet 2007), pornography (Attwood 2007, Mowlabocus 2010) and the display of warmth (Hjorth 2009). This is said, for example, to involve the blurring of play and labour (Petersen 2008, Arora 2011) and it has been noted that the enrolment of personal bonds as becoming integral to the cause and effect of the exchange of material goods (Baker 2012). In respect of SNSs, perhaps the most discussed issues relating to commerce are centred on user data (Hearn 2008, Light et al. 2008, Miller 2008, Everitt and Mills 2009, Fuchs 2010, Lovnik 2011, Gerlitz and Helmond 2013). This again has roots in early work on database marketing, but also that associated with search engines where it has been argued that the information needs of users and their personal data are subject to a growing commercial exploitation (Röhle 2007) and more general deployment of code to sort and order data in order to configure how organisations interact with us (Graham 2004; 2005). However, matters of commerce and SNSs are not restricted to data in the sense crafted via algorithms and in hidden databases, and others have pointed to the potential for listening in such spaces as Twitter. For example, Dell has been cited as a case of a company that has embraced social media by appointing a Vice President of Communities and Conversations (Crawford 2009). Here such listening is concerned with a focus on comment and discussion in Twitter rather than the analysis of the underlying data in terms of social network linkages, for example. Such a view also provokes a question regarding the outcomes of such listening practice and what happens in response. Here, it has been argued that it is too early to tell whether such responses, and more particularly promoted content may affect "regular" discourse in SNSs (Murphy 2013). That said, more broadly, it has been argued that if Web 2.0 develops in accordance with the logic of the marketplace, issues of agency and exclusion will grow in prominence (Bigge 2006, Everitt and Mills 2009, Fuchs 2010). In the final part of this chapter, I want consider disconnective practice in terms of its potential limitations in the context of such commercial aspects of SNSs. Overwhelmingly my participants saw the provision of what they saw as "free services" as something that had to be paid for in some way:

> They have to make money some way and subscription services are a big challenge (look at The Times and Sun pay walls), especially as someone else will offer it for free. I have a Nectar card, a club card, a Boots card – like everyone else I've been bought for discounts so I can buy more – most of us are complicit in some way in perpetuating capitalism. I'm not a capitalist, really, I don't think the free market works very well in practice, but I enjoy many of capitalism's spoils and I don't see that culture changing in the West in my lifetime so if you can't beat them etc... so I'm basically as apathetic as everyone else, but I don't really want to make my own yoghurt or use a moon cup or whatever, and I like having a smartphone and buying more DVDs than I'll ever watch so them's the breaks.
>
> (Denise, media consultant, 25–34)

The trade-off the Denise refers to above was a familiar point of discussion in the interviews, with everyone responding to this subject in much the same way. It was a similar picture irrespective of demographic and even amongst those even who might be regarded as media savvy, like Denise. As Lovnik (2011: 13) states: "This is the price of the free, and we seem more than willing to pay it." The one point that several participants made was that they were generally comfortable with, though sometimes frustrated by, having advertising appear within a site. However, they did not want advertising to dominate their experience, with these people stating that if it did, they would probably stop using a particular space. In-site advertising, particularly that which was seen as targeted, was often presented as an annoyance more than

Table 6.4 How do SNSs make money?

Selling advertising space; from external companies and users who set up pages and chose to "boost" their views by paying to advertise. (Kerry, local government worker, 35–44)

Facebook – advertising, Twitter ads – sponsored posts. (Rebecca, school teacher, 35–44)

Social networking sites like Facebook and Twitter make money through direct advertising and they also collect data about their users and sell it to third parties. (Kevin, sales assistant, 25–34)

Advertising. Banner ad's on Gaydar, Grindr and "suggested pages you may like" on FB. (Wayne, occupational therapist, 45–54)

YouTube has those evil ads that everyone can't wait to hit the skip button on. (Denise, media consultant, 25–34)

YouTube is an interesting example – the inventors/owners are worth billions but the content is mainly contributed by the users/community for free. (Katie, social technologist, 35–44)

Fitlads has advertisements if you are a free member. It makes it money from them or by charging for membership. (Andy, legal professional, 25–34)

Twitter has fewer advertisements but the occasional advert comes up in the feed. (Andy, legal professional, 25–34)

Pages dedicated to a particular item, e.g. games or sportswear that constantly badger you to be "liked" and by doing so spread their influence and reach. (Aleksy, IT analyst, 25–34)

For sites like Gaydar, I know they again use advertising to make money but they also charge for a premium membership. (Simon, Civil Servant, 25–34)

---

anything else. However, it was generally recognised that advertising was the mechanism by which SNS companies made money (Table 6.4).

The quotes presented in Table 6.4 point to various forms of advertising taking place within SNSs that users are aware of including: banner-style advertisements, promoted posts/tweets, in-video advertising and dedicated commercial accounts used by a variety of institutions. Several participants took advantage of such arrangements; particularly those related to the development of entities beyond their personal profile, to promote businesses, hobbies and events they were associated with. Matt, for example, promoted his band and Suzanne, her pet salon and art exhibitions. However, such engagements were not necessarily commercial in nature, as illustrated by Simon:

> the alter ego that I have is purely something that I have for fun, it's not something I do as a business, it's not something I do to make

money, it's something I do purely to enjoy. When it comes down to club nights and things like that, it's the DJ that does all the sharing, I just turn up. It's that kind of thing, so when I say that I use the profile as an advertising thing, it's not really an advertising thing to say "this is the kind of thing I do, you can book me for a party", I mean it as "she'll be going out, if you want to come out and have a night out with her, feel free", because that's the main thing that I do with it, I go out as the alter ego to have a good time, that's the only thing that I do with it. It would be lovely if I did have a job through it, but...

(Simon, civil servant, 25–34)

The participants were also aware of other routes for SNSs to attempt to generate profit. These included, the provision of premium services, which were mostly mentioned in two ways – the additional services provided via premium membership of LinkedIn and those relating to networking sites targeted at gay and bisexual men. A further mode of income generation identified was user data. This was discussed in terms of such things as profile data and interaction data generated by users but also in terms of the generation of content as has been identified of course in other work (Arvidsson 2006, Baym 2009, Arora 2011). It was also noted that some people might not mind being advertised to if the products and services were seen of as appropriate. Moreover, some participants reported that they even engaged in advertising products and services on the behalf of particular companies by giving "shout outs" where good service had been received or if products were seen as cool, or consistent with a users presentation of self. It is interesting to note here that such practices are not specific to a western frame either. Bahfen (2009) lucidly describes the case of Procter and Gamble, who together with two Malaysian partners, launched an official Friendster profile of its Head & Shoulders shampoo brand, targeted at the 16- to 24-year-old age group. The profile, H'n'S Kuala Lumpur, operates via a character of a young woman whose apparent hobbies include "fighting the five signs of dandruff to give you the confidence of flake free, soft, smooth itch-free hair". At the time of writing, Bahfen notes that more than 24,000 people had linked to the profile as a fan. As van Dijck and Poell (2013) argue, recommendation culture grounded in automated connectivity shows a Janus-faced quality where some users appreciate the role of platforms and others loathe it, regarding it as a signal of intruded privacy or commercial exploitation of their user information.

It is also important to note that such shout out's might not be a conscious activity. For instance, in a study of New Zealand youth engagement with alcohol consumption and Bebo use, alcohol brands and their associated marketing teams are shown to take a back seat in such matters. Instead, youth directly integrate such brands into their branding of self to produce "intoxigenic social identity" which positions alcohol consumption as a normative practice amongst youth (Griffiths and Casswell 2010). Through such activity, I argue that the consumers in this case create disconnection which affords the necessary distance alcohol producers may need to have, due to guidelines and laws regarding the responsible consumption of alcohol and direct marketing of products towards young people. Commercial alcohol producers therefore benefit from such disconnective practices. I do not intend to moralise in this respect; however, such activity does raise interesting ethical questions regarding the potential harm and interests present. What we have here is an exercise of power where the consumers of alcohol may lose out by engaging without even realising they are doing so. The first way consumers may lose out is of course due to the potential health effects of binge drinking these youth are argued to be engaging with. The second way consumers may loose out is the potential for hidden audiences and audiences of the future to make judgments about them based on photography of their inebriated exploits. This discussion links well with that which has noted how camera-phone-based self portraiture and photography more generally can mimic mass media conventions and be commodified in the interest of site operators (Cohen 2005, Lee 2005, Cox 2007, Hjorth 2007, Schwarz 2010). However, rather than emphasising the role of connection with photography and commerce, we can see here also how disconnection can play a part.

So far I have emphasised the connective possibilities of SNSs as it relates to their commercial nature. The processes of advertising, data collection and content appropriation are usually, though not always as in the latter example, premised on connectivity. In the next section, I will consider how disconnective practices are deployed in attempt by users to disrupt such connective attempts by SNSs and the other actors who have commercial objectives for them.

Attempting to resist commerce in SNSs

Despite participants being aware that engaging with SNSs was a trade-off and that the spaces they used were inherently commercialised in a variety of ways, some participants did make some attempts to resist what can be seen as the monetisation and or commodification of a variety of aspects of everyday life. At its very simplest, participants reported the provision of minimal or inaccurate personal data. They were aware of discourses regarding the desire of platform owners for transparent and consistent data about themselves and their interactions in their spaces (van Dijck 2013c). They also reported not using SNSs to log into various other online services, as participants were aware that this provided data about their activities that could also be commercialised. That said, the main area of discussion in relation to resisting the commercial advances of SNS providers was in the intertwined area of signifying content preferences and content distribution.

The "Like economy" has created an infrastructure that in one way presents itself as facilitating sociality, but which simultaneously metricises activity. It enables particular kinds of social engagement and creates relations between the social and the marketable (Gerlitz and Helmond 2013). Indeed others have characterised such processes as involving the commercialisation and commodification of interactivity (Bermejo 2009). The participants in the study were aware that devices such as Likes in Facebook have economic value, with Matt particularly suggesting that if you obtain enough likes on a page, this can be sold on as you have effectively built up a valuable marketplace. Participants were also particularly aware that the process of liking contributed to the generation of commercial data and consequently engaged in disconnective practice of a simple kind – choosing not to like:

> No, no. You can get spammed with all sorts that way. Does my head in; I don't bother with it.
>
> > (Tom, retail assistant, 16–24)

> I don't like to be targeted so I am very selective of things that I choose to like.
>
> > (Kerry, local government worker, 35–44)

Moreover, again, rather than using the like, or share function (which was also seen as providing similar data to liking), participants, such as Hannah, reported – "I don't use it they way they want you to" and that she would cut and paste stories herself rather than using automated functions. Hannah, and others who did this, saw this as a way of mediating the amount of data third parties could collect about them. This kind of discussion mostly centred on Facebook, even though other very popular sites such as Twitter and LinkedIn carry advertising which can be shared with others in a similar fashion. A few participants did mention

Twitter, but they were in the minority. In general, participants acknowledged this was not a process that extricated them from commerce completely. Kevin, as he discusses below, even went as far as paying for software to help edit his online presence, but even he acknowledged the limitations he faced.

> Yes, I did recently cull a load that I'd accumulated over the years and just deleted them all. I found a programme which automatically does that for you as well, because I'm aware of all the different ways that all the different companies track you to the point where you could be tracked hundreds of times just being on the internet for 5 minutes, for hundreds of companies just tracking every single thing that you're doing, where you've come from, where you're going to ... I use software to stop websites from tracking my activity online e.g. Facebook monitors which websites you have visited after Facebook even if you logged out of Facebook and then sells this to other companies (or is compelled to give it to the intelligence services). I understand that I'm not completely removing myself from any of this but I do as much as possible and engage as little as possible.
>
> (Kevin, sales assistant, 25–34)

The points Kevin makes above also point to disconnective practice as an ongoing process, here particularly in relation to attempts at resisting the commercial. One might situate such activity in relation to our use pop up blockers and spam filters. This was also made clear by Jyoti and Katie:

> Erm, yeah in a way. Facebook at some point I remember they changed the security settings and then ... you then had to, they basically opened up accounts with their security setting but then you had to go in and change settings back So in some ways, of people knew that but definitely opened for ... I'm sure they do manipulate that kind of thing with all the data they've got on there I'm sure they sell it to advertising companies and ... you know, whoever else.
>
> (Jyoti, sales director, 35–44)

> I really dislike Facebook – their track record in terms of changing privacy settings, not telling users, telling users but making it so damn complicated that many people just don't have the digital literacies to keep up ... Not a fan at all.
>
> (Katie, social technologist, 35–44)

Not only does Katie's point support the idea of disconnective practice being a necessarily continuous process, embedded within it is a point that suggests this it is something that has to be learnt. We can think of it as a digital literacy. Kevin's point above also signals the potential for disconnective practice itself to be commercial in nature – he paid to enact a form of disconnection by attempting to have the tracking associated with him via SNSs and other sites reduced. Therefore, disconnective practice is not just something that we may learn, it is something that, possibly, we may have to learn to pay for.

Conclusions

Personalising the use of SNSs is heavily influenced by the deployment of Goffman's conception of identity. Goffman's (1959) dramaturgical metaphor remains relevant. In particular I am referring to his points regarding our strategies of tailoring self-presentation based on context and audience, and the navigation of front stage and backstage areas. Disconnective practice, I would argue, is integral to this activity of self presentation; it is about attempting to exercise power over as much what we do not present (or connect) as it is that which we do. It is also something that involves other people and things exercising such power in the same respects. Of course, as this chapter demonstrates, there is more to personal use than purely identity work and disconnective practice is integral here whether it is used to lubricate social relations; engage in self-censorship; censorship for the sake of others; make best use of the features of a given SNS; or whether it is being subject to the disconnective effects of SNSs themselves. Indeed, these effects are not limited to the examples I have provided here. The wavering popularity of a platform or the perceived value of a site was also spoken of by participants as playing a part and I have no doubt there will be others. This chapter also demonstrates how disconnection can be enacted in relation to the philosophy of a site, as in the case of Habbo, and how disconnective practice might be engaged to create conceptual distance between that we see as online, and the physical world.

Finally, I also point to the potential limits of disconnective practice where commerce is concerned. Not only do such limits present themselves in terms of the power of the non-human as manifest in algorithms, databases and functions, but also as related to the our apathy and perceived helplessness to resist commercial imperatives. This is perhaps most worryingly present in the idea that we may even have to pay to engage in disconnective practice. This is particularly troublesome when we consider the kinds of disconnection we all might want to have enacted at some point in time. In the closing stages of writing this book I became aware of a case of a woman with considerable mental health problems. She had posted material about an ex-partner to a site dedicated to exacting revenge. She was in a very problematic emotional state when she did this and as her condition improved, she decided she had done the wrong thing and wanted to take the post down. Because she was in such an emotional state when she had originally posted the material, she had not realised that in order to remove material, she had to pay several hundred American dollars to the site owner. This woman does not work because of her health issues and it will take her some time to save the money to pay for the content to be removed.

7
Disclosing Health and Wellbeing

Introduction

In this chapter, I consider how disconnective practice might figure in people's engagements with SNSs as related to health and wellbeing. However to contextualise this, it is important to note that both so called "traditional" and digital media have been enrolled in multiple arguments regarding the potentials for positive and negative affects in this respect. Such arguments relate to both our physical and mental health. In terms of our physical health, we will be aware of screen media in particular as being positioned as turning us into "couch potatoes" for instance. In terms of our mental health, discourses regarding cyber bullying, antisociality and addiction are rife. I am not saying that SNSs cannot have problematic health affects, they can. As I discussed in Chapter 6, nuanced studies of young people's participation with alcohol, binge drinking, commercial branding and identity work demonstrate this is possible (Griffiths and Casswell 2010). However, we now have a wealth of research that demonstrates that social networks are a setting where social support can be experienced and exchanged (Cant 2004) and that even work prior to the development of SNSs suggested that the Internet may help strengthen social networks (Katz and Aspden 1997, Wellman et al. 2001, Kraut et al. 2002). There is also research which suggests that strong social networks can improve health outcomes (Crawford 1987, Lubben and Gironda 1996, Seeman 1996). Therefore, it is perhaps no surprise that contemporary studies demonstrate the potentials of SNSs in this respect. For instance, pro-anorexia groups on SNSs can be geared towards providing social support (Juarascio et al. 2010) and not necessarily harmful as earlier Internet research has suggested (Tiller et al. 1997). SNSs have also been shown to offer support mechanisms for those with disabilities, although it is important to note that participants' dialogues may not be concerned with the disabilities they experience and but rather their experiences and shared interests beyond this (Söderström 2009).

Health and wellbeing service providers also interpret traditional and digital media as key mechanisms for improving us. The role of "traditional" media such as print, radio and TV as deployed in health contexts is well documented and research in this area covers a range of topics which focus very much on the potentials and pitfalls of engaging with them. Key themes here include:

- economic issues – particularly regarding the costs of mass media, and perceived return on investment (Wellings and Macdowall 2000, Elder et al. 2004, Kelly et al. 2005);
- other influences – the effects of activity beyond any given intervention – for example, links between smoking and tobacco taxation, alcohol consumption and commercial advertising of said products (Siegel and Biener 2000, Friend and Levy 2002);
- promotion tactics – to use extreme images or not (Raftopoulou 2007); and
- questions regarding the role of news reporting – the extent to which the media is active in dealing with health issues beyond any superficial engagement with, say, notions of ill health and celebrity (Hilton and Hunt 2010).

Additional work has emerged since the 1990s which focuses more on digital media in the light of developments relating to home computing, mobile media and, of course, the Internet. In terms of themes here we see areas such as:

- cost reduction – the ability of the digital to mitigate the increasing cost burdens of delivering healthcare and pressures on resources (Brock and Smith 2007, Kaldo et al. 2008, Muñoz 2010, Riper et al. 2011) and shifts to exploit the resources of patients themselves via digital media (Hejlesen et al. 2001);
- qualitative improvement – arguments are made that digital media maybe more clinically effective than traditional modes of intervention for particular conditions (Brendryen and Kraft 2008, Kahol 2011);
- improved accessibility – digital media are argued to afford potentially 24 hours a day access and pacing of treatment to suit individuals'

needs and lifestyles (Strecher 2007, Gomez 2008, Rice et al. 2012, Rini et al. 2012);

- increased interactivity – digital media are considered to offer much more scope for public engagement than the mass media (Turner-McGrievy et al. 2009, Ito and Brown 2010); and
- anonymity – especially for those seeking advice about more sensitive health topics (Rice 2006, Valenzuela et al. 2007, Turner-McGrievy et al. 2009, Ito and Brown 2010).

Some researchers also point to potential challenges for digital media. Some report problems of willingness and ability of healthcare providers to invest in implementing digital media health services (Viswanath and Kreuter 2007, Ito and Brown 2010, Evers et al. 2013, Korda and Itani 2013); issues concerned with perceived credibility of the Internet (Gray et al. 2005a) and indeed those formal institutions who may have credibility due to brand name recognition, but who may not do a very good job of creating credible and engaging sites, particularly where young people are concerned (Eysenbach 2008). Somewhat tied to the issue of credibility is that of a lack of media literacy – it has been suggested that this can affect the quality of online experiences (Gray et al. 2005b, Gray and Klein 2006).

The literature to date, regarding engagement with SNSs for health and wellbeing is nascent. As with much SNS research an emphasis on connection runs through much of this body of work, and indeed that pre-dating SNSs. In this chapter, I want to consider the extent to which health and wellbeing issues are engaged with via SNSs and the role that disconnective practice can play in this respect. In order to do this I will consider issues associated with users accessing health information, sharing health information and receiving health information.

Accessing health information

All participants in the study were comfortable using the Web in relation to health and wellbeing. The first thing people talked about was using search engines, and Google (or as some termed it "Dr Google") in particular, to look for information about health conditions, to understand what symptoms could be or to find details of where health services could be accessed. Sites such as Web MD, NHS Direct and Wikipedia were also seen as a valuable source of information for some and domain names such as .gov were used as badges of quality – a signifier of a site that could be trusted. Here, as has been suggested by Halavais (2012), we see connectivity being enabled via the consistency of a perception of function (in this case a quality hallmark) that is associated with a particular badge. Such badges can have multiple meanings whereby the quality hallmark associated with a .gov site, may have a brand that resonates with a given audience, may also be seen as lacking credibility by some groups. Yet despite this, the idea of getting access to accurate information that was easy to interpret in a sensible fashion was mentioned by all participants in the study with many explicitly, and jokingly, making the point that if you looked hard enough, you would find that you had a terminal illness. As Rebecca stated: "You know when you're ill you Google it, then you decide you're dying."

More specifically, when asked about SNSs as related to health and wellbeing, initially at least, participants did not think of them as related to such spaces, instead referring more generally to the Web as I have already mentioned. When probed further about this, as to why SNSs was not instantly seen as a mode by which they might engage in activity related to health and wellbeing, it became clear that for some participants, they were not seen as sites of sourcing quality information. As intimated by prior work regarding the Internet and health education (Gray et al. 2005a, 2005b, Gray and Klein 2006, Eysenbach 2008, Evers et al. 2013), disconnective practice therefore was enrolled where there was a perceived lack of credibility. For example, Hannah said she would not use SNSs as she "would probably get just a load of idiots giving me rubbish information" and Jenny responded that: "I'm not friends with any qualified doctors so I wouldn't post 'I've got this weird thing, what do you reckon it is' ".

Participants also saw SNSs as spaces that were for relationship maintenance rather than for engaging with health and wellbeing (even though of course maintaining relationships with others can have health benefits). Initially then, participants reported not connecting with health information with SNSs. However, despite several participants saying that they did not see SNSs as sites of quality health information, the issue of sharing information within such spaces was raised. Rebecca, for example, stated: "I didn't know you could, but no. I wouldn't even think about it." Aleksy's experience was the same, and Suzanne elaborated:

> I don't bother with it. I ignore it. If I want to find something out I'd find it out, sort of, I just don't use Facebook for anything like that. I have seen things where people put warnings, police put warnings for female drivers or if you see certain things. I know people put that

on, which I read then. I can't think of anything else. I know they do put things up like lose a stone in a day, things like that. Get a facelift, they do put things on, don't they, to sort of tap into that.

(Suzanne, pet salon owner, 35–44)

However, all participants had experienced health and wellbeing issues in some way via SNSs, as is shown by Suzanne, whether this was through their actions or those of people they were connected with in any given space. Indeed a key SNS discussed was YouTube; this was highlighted as being incredibly helpful for learning about conditions and also following surgical procedures to gain an understanding of what might take place. For example, Simon reported that he had been looking on YouTube for videos for people that had undergone eye surgery to see how well they were recovering from it because there was a possibility that he would need it in the near future. This involved, as has been discussed earlier in the book, lurking activity which did not require Simon to make explicit his activity, offering him an opportunity to engage in disconnective practice. Wayne (an occupational therapist), also reported using SNSs to get basic knowledge regarding a health matter he was not familiar with at work, as a "way in" to the more complicated more formal knowledge he would then access via what he saw as more traditional sources such as books.

Other disconnective practice enrolled to access health information included the use of backchannels to ask friends about health and wellbeing issues. Here, for example, Andy asked friends who went to the gym about symptoms that developed every time he went and Kerry asked someone she knew, who was a professional singer, how they dealt with throat problems. Even though disconnective practices were enrolled in each of these cases, an element of experience, and credibility, is also enrolled – these participants made judgements about who and what to access.

Sharing health information

A significant area of discussion was the extent to which participants would share their health status within SNSs and their interpretations of others doing the same. One line of discussion here was the idea that people would only share what they saw as mundane illness updates – nothing too serious. For example, Nina said she might: "moan about health issues like 'oh I've got a really sore toe', I might tweet that" and

Ela said she might post because she would "want people to pity me for a bit...." Although, others were ready to sit in judgment on such status updates:

> Attention seeking. People saying "oh I'm so ill", it just gets on my nerves.
>
> (Sarah, call centre worker, 16–24)

Sarah's comment is emblematic of more general comments made by people in the study regarding over-sharing and prior work which has also highlighted those who engaging in such activity as being a subject of particular scorn and humour (Hargittai et al. 2012). Other examples of such mundane health updates included the linking of exercise apps with SNS accounts to display personal progress, details of any minor accidents (a picture for instance showing the results of falling off a bike) and enquiries regarding how to treat such injuries. However, these were all played down very much as only happening where things were very minor and mundane.

The sharing of health information was significantly shaped by people's conceptions of whether it was relevant or not to do so. This question of relevance was nuanced in different ways. For example, Kevin would only share news items from institutions if it was read as a "scientific breakthrough" and deemed to be of relevance to a wider population. For others, another moderator of relevance was the extent to which the information was seen as accurate or helpful. In respect of personal health information, participants reported not feeling that it was relevant to share such data generally as they felt people would not be interested. However, when asked, some reported that they would respond to people's enquiries, depending upon the nature of what they were asking about. Disconnective practice as self-editing was very much at play in respect of sharing health information and, as shown in other parts of this book, sharing too much irrelevant information was seen as an inappropriate thing to do. This analysis adds to discussions of relevance and SNSs by going beyond the association of relevance and disconnection in terms of discourses of technological progress of the "why people left MySpace" kind (Bull 2010, Ralph et al. 2011). That is, a lack of perceived relevance may not necessarily lead to leaving a space, especially if one is talking about particular content. It may of course be another matter if the whole SNS becomes irrelevant.

Another reason for not sharing information about one's health status was concerned with SNSs not being seen as the right place to do this in much the same way it reportedly wasn't the right place to access information about health:

> I don't think Facebook is a place where you should go to share your health problems, because I think it is a personal thing, health, and... I do know one friend a few months ago put on that she just lost a baby that night, and that, as sorry as I was, I didn't know this person very well, she was from school... as sorry as I was the first thought I had was "it's awful that the first thing you thought of doing when you found out was putting it on Facebook and letting everyone read about it" and I disagreed with that. I don't think it's a place where you should be doing that. Keep it personal; keep it private, that's what I say.
>
> (Bob, cleaner, 25–34)

> Yeah, if I've suffered really badly then I'd feel it's not the place to advertise it. I've got a friend who's, she's just being diagnosed with breast cancer, she's not put anything on about it. One of her sons has took a photo of her in a wig because she's just obviously lost all her hair through her chemo, but there's no mention of it; no mention of it on her status. She's got a lot of people who know, everyone's been quite tactful. I think there's certain things you shouldn't put on about your health. [Unclear]. But yeah, yeah, some people do go into graphic detail about stuff, but I don't put anything about my health. Occasionally, if I've had D&V or a cold...
>
> (Julie, health care assistant, 35–44)

Here, participants suggest that health and wellbeing are private matters not to be shared with SNSs, even though they have experiences of people undertaking that activity. Indeed, where some participants experience health information sharing that is deemed too much for such spaces (as for example Bob's friend who had lost a baby and posted about this) it can be read negatively. In contrast, the fact that Julie's friend had not posted about her serious ill health was commended. Disconnective practice is again shown to be morally charged and interpreted. Julie's friend did "the right thing" by choosing not to publicise her problems, whereas Bob's friend was questioned for doing so. Editorial ethics also extended to what was deemed appropriate to share on other people's behalf, as Kerry explained:

Erm...I think if you're talking about yourself on somebody's [wall] it's alright, but you shouldn't talk about other people's health. So, you know, I wouldn't...if some people put "How's your mother in law doing?" I'd text them back; I wouldn't reply on Facebook, you know, because it's not appropriate, so I suppose it...if people are careful what they put, then fair enough, you know.

(Kerry, local government worker, 35–44)

Beyond the mundane

One area where SNSs were potentially seen as helpful by participants was as related to the personal management of long term conditions (such as Parkinson's disease, anorexia or Alzheimer's disease) or the provision of support for those who cared for people in such a situation. To clarify, in such discussions, this involved nearly all participants reporting that they did not have such a condition but that they could see value for those who did. Moreover, this discussion very much blurred SNSs with other sites such as forums and websites akin to PatientsLikeMe. Indeed, people actively referred to forums beyond SNSs as preferred way to access health support:

So it's a little bit different, it feels different. I usually don't post on forums but I read it in terms of checking what's available and I suppose if people were actually posting on it and that would feed automatically into their Facebook or Twitter account, then I'm not sure. Somehow, it feels more private on a forum and obviously you don't use your normal name or anything.

(Ela, translator, 25–34)

Forums yes, that kind of social networking online community, I would read. I wouldn't necessarily participate that much but I would read them yes.

(Kevin, sales assistant, 25–34)

Where SNSs were talked about specifically, these participants framed this in terms of having access to forum type functionality within such spaces. The idea here was that people could connect with each other but in private. Privacy, in particular, was emphasised by Wayne (a health professional) as was the notion of consent:

I think if it was a specific group of clients or patients that had it and it was a support network or an information sharing thing between

all of those people, I think that's absolutely fine because you've all
agreed to be in part of the group haven't you?

(Wayne, occupational therapist, 45–54)

For many participants, the management of a long-term condition was
not necessarily seen as something for public consumption in much the
same ways as I have already outlined for other health conditions in this
chapter. Indeed other research has suggested that the ability to craft private spaces that are closed and unsearchable has also been positioned as
a reason for why those with certain conditions, such as anorexia, choose
SNS sites to create spaces of support (Juarascio et al. 2010). However,
for others with long-term conditions, the situation can be very different. During the study I was able to briefly interview Val, a person who
lives with a bleeding disorder. Her deteriorating condition has meant
she has needed to retire from work in her early 40s after working full
time since leaving school at 18. Val was actively part of a number of
groups on Facebook which were, as other participants identified, closed
and could only be accessed via approval from an administrator. Here
such disconnective practice was enrolled to all those who engaged a
degree of privacy regarding their personal health status. However, Val
also stated that she used her own personal accounts on Facebook and
Twitter to raise awareness about her condition. She did this by posting
photographs of bleeds that she experienced to demonstrate the sever-
ity and debilitating nature of her condition. When I asked her about
why she chose to publicly present others with the details of the condition, she told me that she was "fed up of people giving her grief for
not working anymore" and "wanted them to see what it was like for
her having to live with a bleeding disorder – day in, day out". Therefore, whist disconnective strategies might be enrolled for people with
long term conditions, others might choose to reject this approach in
favour of communicating with others in order to attempt educate, shape
opinion and display anger in relation to how they have been treated by
others. As Murphy has suggested, although in many cases, celebrities
and traditional media have overwhelming voice and influence, in some
cases, such as health communities, individual patients can be viewed
as authorities whose voice Twitter has helped make legitimate (Murphy
2013).

Some participants also thought that SNSs could be used to facilitate
better health where people have certain problems because they offer
the chance to connect with others, gain support and even potentially
improve the quality of their lives:

Motorcycle Junction, it's a bit like Facebook, you have a profile and you can make friends on there and chat on there. . . . So I met a guy from Bradford who'd . . . he didn't drink but was an alcoholic . . . But he were nuts; mental! But it were my alcoholism too, but he sort of ticked all the boxes. He had tattoos, the bike, but he didn't drink. That ended in a few months. Then I met a guy on Motorcycle Junction from Glasgow, erm, and he was Cocaine Jack. He got me to AA. Ooop!

(Julie, health care assistant, 35–44)

However, some also mentioned that one would have to be careful as some health conditions, particularly those related to mental health, could actually be made worse by engagement with SNSs. It was also made clear by some that certain conditions and experiences with health consequences might not be taken seriously and that could also lead to problems:

I think it's a bit different because mental health issues are not particularly talked about anyway so, I mean people might be more inclined to do that because talking about it with strangers might be easier than talking about it with people that you know. But I would say I personally wouldn't because it's sensitive issues and if you say something about a problem you're having and someone was to dismiss that or be negative about it that can make a mental health matter so much worse. . . . so if someone was having a support group for people on the internet who had lost their mothers, it's a bit different than a rape support group because people on the internet are not that great about rape and they'd be like "you weren't raped, you're just an idiot". Whereas if someone's mum's dead, they can't be like "your mum's not dead, you're just an idiot". But they're both sensitive issues that people might seek out support for, but people on the Internet are mean.

(Nina, sales assistant, 16–24)

Other studies have also pointed to more general wellbeing problems arising from sharing information. Baughman, for instance, has argued that personal information – both held by the site provider and posted either by a user or by friends and family of a user – can become a source of vulnerability for victims of domestic violence (Baughman 2010). However, it is not just the fact that the person subject to violence is sharing information; as Baughman goes on to explain, it can also be that the abusive partner may share information. In the case of Rios v Fergusan in North Carolina, Fergusan posted a video of himself rapping on YouTube that showed him waving a gun and threatening to harm Rios. According to Baughman, in his video, Fergusan rapped about wanting to shoot Rios and put her face on the dirt until she can't breathe no more".

Another area of discussion regarding the creation of other problems related to information sharing with SNSs was how this was perceived to relate to health and wellbeing, or not:

> I think there was a case about a year ago of this woman putting a picture of her with an amputated breast or something like that, saying that "I've defeated cancer" and stuff like that and "you should get yourself checked out because you will die", and the picture got removed off Facebook and there was a big uproar about it, people saying "well it was there in a positive way, and it's isn't offending".
>
> (Aleksy, IT analyst, 25–34)

Here, the SNSs provider engaged in disconnective practice by engaging an editorial ethics, arguably very much taking content out of context and based on parameters that are heteronormative, contradictory and controversial. The presence of photographs of women's breasts (and arguably, more specifically, their nipples) in general in Facebook is disallowed. An underlying assumption here is that it is not appropriate for such parts of a woman's body to be public in that space or only under certain terms (Facebook seems to have very little problem with photographs of glamour models with heaving chests and scantily clad in bikinis within the site). The contradiction here of course is that it is perfectly acceptable for men's breasts and nipples to be in public view (even if a woman is touching them – but it frequently becomes more problematic if it is another man). Another set of issues identified, were those where concerns were raised for others in someone's network. Kevin, for instance, said he would be very wary about posting about common serious conditions such as cancer because it is likely that someone he knew would have direct experience of it and he would not want to upset them.

Receiving health information from institutions

Another aspect of experiencing health and wellbeing information sources with SNSs related to the reception of health and wellbeing related news generated by institutions rather than individuals. This included such things as news stories from other spaces on the Web, and those found within a given space – in a newsfeed on Facebook or a stream in Twitter, for example. Moreover, as I mentioned at the beginning of this chapter, in recent years, the connectivity associated with SNSs has been seen as something to be exploited by providers of health and wellbeing services. This has led to engagements with SNSs in a variety of contexts with aims such as awareness raising, knowledge building and increasing confidence about a range of health and wellbeing issues. In the UK, some of the most prominent areas of engagement have been related to various forms of cancer and sexual health. Sexual health has been seen as an area particularly ripe for engagement because it is often associated with young people and young people are associated with SNSs. That said the extent to which SNS-based interventions are desired or indeed effective is still subject to debate. Across the participants in this study, the extent to which participants would engage with such connective attempts was variable. Again here, the issue of relevance surfaced. In one way, such relevance was moderated by a perception of the kinds of content that people wanted to see in their feed or stream:

> Even though it can be a good cause, obviously like cancer research is important, but if you imagine you open your Facebook up and the first 20 pages were about cancer research with the same picture, you're going to get annoyed about it eventually.
>
> (Aleksy, IT analyst, 25–34)

My view was also moderated by a perception that doing things online was not seen as an activity that was going to translate into something concrete. This lack of material impact was used as a way to argue that it was not relevant to engage with connective attempts of institutions (and the individuals that supported them) in terms of health campaigning:

> ...what's sharing it on Facebook going to do, there's plenty of other ways of raising awareness and those things like "like this if you're against cancer", great what's that going to do. It's not actually doing anything positive. If I wanted to raise awareness I would do something like fundraising or something proactive rather than just posting a status about it.
>
> (Jenny, school teacher, 25–34)

Jenny further drove home her point by stating that she would only really engage with something where there was some material impact. Here she gave the example of sharing a link to a Just Giving page by someone running a marathon to raise money for a health cause. Consequently, the connectivity health institutions might aim to appropriate for their own ends might be resisted where there is a perceived lack of material impact. Disconnective practice therefore might be engaged as a mode of determining relevance.

Case study: What's not to love about cats on the Internet?

In this section, I want to share a case study that introduces other mediators which can affect people's engagement with the connective attempts of those working with and for health institutions. I was part of a digital-media-based project aimed at trying to engage first-time invitees to cervical screening (pap smear) appointments – in the UK this means women aged 25–29 (see (Light and Ormandy 2013)). Based on prior research, the potentials for social media and humour as applicable to this area had been established (Light and Ormandy 2011), and informed by engagement with the target group, a digital media campaign related to cats, a staple of Internet meme culture, was created. The campaign comprised a central presence on Facebook, a campaign website, a Twitter account, a YouTube channel and a Pinterest account. These were used to host and circulate a range of content developed to promote the campaign such as mashups, existing cat images circulating the web, a Mogatron app and a series of videos featuring cats.

Determining the overall success of the campaign is problematic as there is a lack of data available from previous campaigns to understand this in context. That said, based on a self-reporting survey 52.8% of women who had not gone for a screening before, reported that they now would. The campaign was generally reported as being effective at raising awareness, knowledge and confidence with respect to the need for cervical screening also. It was praised for its clear, humorous approach and appropriate tone. In many ways then, the connective attempts made with SNSs could be said to be have been successful. Women in the target age group, and indeed those outside of it, connected with the campaign. Consequently, while in this chapter I have pointed to a somewhat of a lack of interest in institutional attempts at connections, there does also seem to be some appetite for this. That said, through our focus groups, survey and within SNSs, we received feedback from women that they would not connect with the campaign. The reason women would not connect with the campaign was that they either did not understand why cats were being used or because they did not have an affective association with cats.

As referred to in Chapter 6 in respect of the non-engagement with likes, cats can be interpreted as generating disconnection because they do not command an affective association with the person/s in question. In terms of further explaining this state of affairs, I need to expand on two points. First, there is the issue of a lack of understanding of why cats were being used. Here, we had women who were not familiar with Internet meme culture (even with the 25–29 age group) and could not reconcile the serious nature of cervical cancer with the humour being presented to them via the campaign. However, this was a minor point. From the outset, it was recognised by the team, that some women would not engage with the campaign. More importantly, women reported not understanding why we had used cats, even when they were aware of memes such as lolcats. Part of this lack of understanding was the fact we were trying to do something that was unexpected, but also it was due to the loss of meaning originally embedded in the name of the campaign. Originally, the campaign name had been chosen by women in the target group and was the playfully risqué and tongue in cheek – Happy Healthy Pussy. However, upon consultation with other parties, the campaign name was eventually changed to "The Cat That Got The Screen" in order that no one would be offended. For many women, this change of name meant they lost the meaning of the con-nection between cats and the campaign and consequently they found it hard to connect with the campaign itself. The second point, that concerned the affective association with cats, was raised as a reason by a minority of women in the study. Generally those who said they didn't really like cats reported that they still thought the campaign was good, but not for them. However, more significantly, a strand of the project was to develop understandings of south Asian women's experi-ences of cervical screening and their preferences for campaigns. In this instance, the south Asian women we spoke with defined themselves as being of Indian, Pakistani and Bangladeshi origin. These women were represented in the initial development of the campaign but upon engagement with a broader cross-section of this group via a series of focus groups it became clear that cats would not work for many of them. In contrast to the other women who did not like cats, these women explained that cats were just not part of their culture. It was therefore not a question of liking them or not, they were not seen as cuddly, humorous animals that were engaging to humans. Therefore, on the basis of this cultural position, these women positioned the theme of the campaign as something that would not connect with them. Overall then we see that the content of health campaigns themselves can affect the extent to which people might choose to connect, and moreover that such disconnective practice may be influenced by cultures beyond that of the SNSs in question.

Case study: A failure to disconnect with death in Ghana?

In this final section of this chapter, I will draw on some work of John Effah. This case study has been developed in conjunction with John based on my interest in disconnection and his interest in dotcom entrepreneurship in Ghana (Effah 2011, Effah and Light 2012, Effah 2014). It represents a case of part of perhaps the ultimate disconnection we might have with SNSs – when we die.

In Ghana, funerals are important social events. Among Ghanaians death is an occasion for family and community reunion. In addition to family, members of the deceased's community, such as neighbours, friends and work colleagues and their families, are expected to attend funerals as guests. The funeral usually lasts three days, beginning with a vigil on Friday night as the corpse is publicly displayed amidst music, singing and colourful decorations. On Saturday morning, a church service is conducted for the dead after which the body is conveyed in a procession to the graveyard for burial. In the afternoon, a grand durbar is organised in an open space. Guests are entertained with music, drinks and food; in return they are expected to donate to the bereaved family, helping to pay the costs incurred. On Sunday morning, a thanksgiving church service is organised. In the afternoon, the durbar continues so that guests who could not attend on the Saturday can pay their respects. On the following Monday, the family meets to settle the financial accounts of the funeral, declaring a profit or loss.

Funerals are socially and symbolically significant for the people of Ghana. They serve as an occasion to strengthen social and family ties, bringing together Ghanaians at home and abroad (Mazzucato et al. 2006). The occasion has also been described as "dating market" for people (de Witte 2001, Mazzucato et al. 2006). Moreover, funerals afford families the opportunity to showcase their status and wealth in order to retain or upgrade their prestige in society (de Witte 2003). Throughout the funeral, guests pay keen attention to the conduct and performance of the bereaved family, and expect to be impressed (Bonsu and DeBerry-Spence 2008). Funerals also afford an opportunity to demonstrate the status of the dead. One can measure the social status of the dead from the number of attendees, the quality of coffin and the decorations used. Prestigious, enlarged and framed photographs of the dead are also exhibited to demonstrate their social status. Further, relatives wear badges, T-shirts and clothes printed with photographs of the deceased. Moreover, pictures of the dead, the attendees and the events in general, in addition to video-recordings, are collected for later distribution. Funerals in Ghana are imbued with social networks and networking activity.

Influenced by seeing the role of digital networks in developed counties, Ray, an entrepreneur saw a potential in creating a site of networking for funerals. His intention was to reduce the costs of celebrating funerals by working with families to provide cheaper access to advertising media as well as recording relevant information about the celebration. Normally, Ghanaian funerals, involved the expenditure of much time and money in expectation of high attendance. Families have to pay for expensive radio, television and newspaper funeral announcements and advertisements. Moreover, they spend a lot of money on posters, invitations and thank-you cards. Some families have even enrolled billboards, showing the picture of the deceased, and which function as invitations to invite guests to funerals. The size and quality of billboards perform symbolically to emphasise the social status of the deceased and their families. Ray saw his site, as being accessible to bereaved families, service providers and the general public. Families would have their announcements and other information uploaded on the website. In addition, they would have the opportunity to create a profile for the deceased where tributes, photos and videos could be uploaded. Also, service providers for funerals would advertise and transact with customers through the network. For this, the site would be linked to their websites to provide access to visitors. Ray initially planned that public access to the website would be free and later people would be asked to pay once they had become enrolled in the network. Moreover, he planned that the service providers would register and pay to get their websites connected to the network, pay for a monthly subscription and for advertisements.

The Internet connected the network to the Ghanaian diaspora – particularly those in the USA, UK and other parts of Europe who encountered it while browsing on the Internet or who were recommended it by friends. The funeral website began to serve as a relief for the diaspora who reported that they could now plan for funerals without leaving their country of residence. The network was described as a vehicle for making all the necessary contacts and arrangements for funeral preparation without necessarily travelling to Ghana. They only had to attend the funeral after making the necessary preparations online. After the funeral, the site offered them the opportunity to showcase photos, videos and tributes to their friends across the world. Before this, those organising the funeral had to video all the events and send the tape to their relatives and friends abroad who could not attend. According to Ray, the Ghanaian diaspora have been key in how the network has evolved as they have requested more tools to support audio and video resources, information sharing among users and self-service facilities.

The network commenced business by offering free services to bereaved families as well as to local service providers. The free service attracted a number of visitors to the network. Bereaved families began to upload obituaries, announcements, photos, videos and related documents for free. The Internet further contributed to promoting the network to the Ghanaian diaspora and Ray was surprised to find out that the network attracted the diaspora more than local customers whom he had originally targeted. Increasingly, affluent Ghanaian residents in the country and the diaspora continued to use the network more than anyone else. These groups used it to showcase their opulence and social status. The more general local population that Ray expected to use network, as an opportunity to reduce their cost of celebrating funerals, seemed less interested.

The response to the network from the Ghanaian public in general forced the Ray to consider alternative strategies to attract more local customers. The first strategy involved issuing a funeral print newspaper. In mid 2009, the organisation introduced a free bi-weekly print newspaper on funerals in Ghana to direct public attention to the opportunities offered by the funeral website. According to Ray, his goal was to use the newspaper as a device to create public awareness in order to attract more local customers and visitors to the website. Electronic copies of the newspaper were also made available online for free download. Although Ray's initial intention was just to create local awareness for the network, the print newspaper has attracted the attention of people in Ghana more than the network. The newspaper was welcomed because it was freely distributed. The general local population could only access the Internet in cafes in big cities, and possibly at their place of work, and this limited their ability for engagement with the network. Another strategy that the organisation has used to expand is by providing ancillary services such as publishing funeral materials and videoing funeral events. Despite Ray's original intention for the company, the persistent requests from people in Ghana to print funeral-related materials such as invitations, thank-you cards and posters forced him to extend it into such physical services. As part of these physical activities, the organisation now provides commercial advice and printing services to bereaved families on activities such as drafting and designing obituaries, tributes, brochures and more. The company also provides video-recording services.

Whilst the network connects with the diaspora and the wealthy local population, it is also important to recognise those on the periphery or those who do not become enrolled. Those without much wealth do not engage because their access to the Internet is restricted to work and expensive cafés. Even though such people might save money in the long run, connections with extant cultures of funerals in Ghana remain. Continuity regarding the culture of Ghanaian funerals with respect to the need/desire to demonstrate status through high payment for services is important here. Such a consideration requires us to consider the materiality of technology and the extent to which it can be seen to have the same symbolic and economic power as physical artefacts. Indeed in this case we also see that geography and politics play a part in mediating the financial value of the digital – the diaspora and wealthier Ghanaians engaged with the network to further promote how much they had spent. The diaspora effectively saw the financial gain in terms of being able to save money with respect to travel costs and time away from work – hidden costs in the funeral. Interestingly, the local Ghanaians who did not earn so much ignored the network's advances and did not see the value of this (as they too could have benefited). They seemed to be subject to hegemony as far as what constituted a good funeral was concerned – it was in their interest to take advantage of the hidden economies to be had (albeit – they would not be as extensive as for those in the diaspora). Power was exerted over them and by them upon each other (and by companies) to do things that were not in their interest – this is despite the attempts of the network to open their eyes to the situation. The performance of Ghanaian funerals was just too strong and was further supported by a lack of access to the Internet – it was taken out of Ray's hands and disconnective practice was enacted.

Conclusion

In this chapter, I have considered the extent to which health and wellbeing issues are engaged with via SNSs and the role that disconnective practice can play in this respect. In order to do this I have discussed issues that are fundamentally associated with users accessing health information, sharing health information and receiving health information. To be clear, of course the connective possibilities play out in this arena, through users sharing mundane updates about their health, operating politically to shape people's understandings of living with long-term health conditions or, for instance, though the deployment of social media campaigns by health and wellbeing oriented institutions. However, it is also clear that disconnective practice is an integral part of doing health and wellbeing with SNSs. In terms of accessing health and wellbeing information, the participants in this study demonstrate how disconnective practice can be enrolled to deal with information and source credibility, how it is present in back channel use for accessing personal networks and how it is manifest in lurking to acquire knowledge of health procedures. Disconnective practice also plays out in relation to the mediation of practices of health and wellbeing information sharing. Here, self editing takes place by users in their attempts to craft relevant networks for those they engage with and in doing so we see how relevance and disconnection regarding SNSs can be associated with other things beyond fashion-based networking switching. It is also clear there can be a psychological element to disconnective practice whereby content and sites are not thought of as appropriate for particular matters. Disconnection also is at play in order to create safe, private, spaces, within broader networks, for those with shared health and wellbeing concerns. The creation of such spaces can also be linked with some people's perceptions that health and wellbeing are private matters, even to the extent that the sharing of some information is deemed to be morally questionable. Importantly, it is not just users who determine morality, SNS providers are engaging with this too. Disconnective practice in relation to information sharing might also be mediated by a health condition itself both in terms of the affect that engaging with SNSs might have on a person's health and in terms of how others might exacerbate that condition if it is revealed within a network. Finally, in terms of the information reception, relevance again can mediate users' disconnective practices as related to institutional attempts at engaging with SNSs. Here such relevance has been shown to potentially involve questions regarding the over sharing of information and also the extent to which such engagements are perceived to have material impact. In addition, I demonstrate how culture can affect engagement whether this is concerned with particular messages and their lack of affective association or because extant arrangements eschew the enrolment of SNSs on particular terms.

There is a wealth of previous research which has interrogated traditional and digital media in relation to its impact on our physical and mental health both in terms of how this might operate informally as we use such media, and how interventions, made by health and wellbeing professionals, might affect us. Over the past few years, this work has begun to encompass SNSs. Whilst this work is nascent, I would argue that it is often couched in terms of tapping into the connective emphasis more generally associated with analyses of SNSs. However, the experiences of the participants in the study, and in the case studies I present here, suggest that a further nuancing of such approaches is necessary whereby the possibilities for disconnective practice are acknowledged and engaged with.

Part IV
Conclusions

8
Towards a Theory of Disconnective Practice

The importance of connection and disconnection

> Social network sites (SNSs) provide a new way to organize and navigate an egocentric social network. Are they a fad, briefly popular but ultimately useless? Or are they the harbingers of a new and more powerful social world, where the ability to maintain an immense network – a social "super net" – fundamentally changes the scale of human society?
>
> (Donath 2007b: 231)

In the quote above, Judith Donath astutely asks both us and herself about the longevity of SNSs and the extent to which they will affect our everyday lives. Early in 2014, almost seven years away from the publication of Donath's paper, and as I write the conclusion to this text, one might say that in some respects the question still stands. I agree with Burgess (2014) that social media platforms, and SNSs, have been incrementally and inexorably made over for the entirety of their existence. This continues to be the case, and as my research participants have alluded to, this is a constant source of both problems and possibilities for connection. SNSs seem to be constantly be attempting to provide new ways to organise and navigate our social networks. At the very least SNSs are being sold to us on the basis of new features. Are they a fad, briefly popular but ultimately useless? On the question of them being a fad, I am not sure – it depends upon what timeframe we are talking about. Are they ultimately useless? Well, I think the past ten years of their existence and our academic research demonstrates the potential for both utility and a lack of it where SNSs are concerned. Overall though, one would most probably have to position them as having utility. However contestable such notions of usefulness might be, SNSs can be said to provide employment, the potential for relational development, the development of social capital, fun, sex and a whole manner of other contributions to our everyday lives. Have they changed the scale of human society? In February 2014, Facebook currently has over 1.2 billion active users per month, Twitter over 240 million active users per month, LinkedIn around 250 million active users, Instagram 150 million active users per month and YouTube has more than 1 billion unique users each month. I think despite these hefty figures, it is still too early to tell the extent of the impact these particular sets of arrangements will have. It may be the likes of Facebook, Twitter or YouTube that stays the course and becomes the ultimate social utility, it maybe something else like them, or something seemingly completely different. I am not one for making predictions. I think what we can say though is that digitally mediated connection has become integral to the lives of many people where it was not so previously. Moreover, these connection arrangements are, and will continue to be, rooted in what has gone before. The extent to which these roots are merely glimmers of older technological arrangements, akin to the links made between telegraph wires, railway tracks and roads (Jones 1997), or whether these are more concretely apparent, as Baym (2007) points to the co-presence of sites such as blogs, social networks, discussion forums and private messaging, in her study of online Swedish rock group fandom, I do not know. Whatever arrangements come into being, I agree with Baym (2009) on the value of a continued emphasis on historically linking our theory, framing and research enquiries. This is something that I have attempted in this text.

Disconnection is, of course, not a new phenomenon that has arisen as mechanism for navigating SNSs. Disconnection it also not something that is specific to SNSs either. The word "disconnection" is a verb, and implies the removal or breaking of connection. It is also a state something can exist in. For my purposes, the practices of disconnection are something that therefore relate to the maintenance of that state and the creation of that state. Although disconnection implies the breaking of a connection, and consequently that a connection has already being made, disconnection as a state can also exist in its own right, in relationship to connection as a possibility. A theory of disconnective practice therefore helps us to understand how states of disconnection come into being with SNSs and how they are maintained. This position is therefore not about just one practice to fit all scenarios, but is a suite of activity involving a variety of people and things, as I shall now elaborate.

Geographies of disconnection

Disconnective practice is situated and one therefore must think of the sites one is concerned with. I think of these sites of disconnection as involving the creation and/or maintenance of disconnection in four ways:

1. With an SNS – at the most basic level, disconnection may translate into non-use where someone chooses, or is precluded from engaging with a particular site. The position may be of variable length.

2. Within a single SNS – this may involve choosing not to connect with people or the functions and features of a given space. This can happen before or after a connection takes place or has taken place. Examples of such practices here are processes of friending, defriending, friend culling, rejection of follow requests, the hiding of posts, the hiding of online status, the use of back channels like private messaging and the enactment of functions that stem heavy friending practices, and the use of sites without engaging their networking affordances (as archives of addresses or as read-only media, for instance).

3. Between an SNS and another SNS, website or application offering or attempting connection – this range of practice can involve such things as choosing not to connect accounts between sites, rebuffing the possibility for logging into another site or application using the login credentials of a site and using social-sharing features inscribed within sites beyond the SNS in question.

4. Between SNSs and spaces of the physical world – these practices include not using an SNS in physical space (due for example to concerns about safety, privacy or social etiquette). It may involve creating a site of disconnection in order to be able to use an SNS in public via the enrolment of physical distance, objects and bodies. The intention here might be to create a private sphere of interaction (Papacharissi 2010), but also it might be used in other ways, including for the performance of activities which are not aimed at socialising with others. Disconnection here might also occur by turning off location services inscribed into a given SNS and the non-completion of geographic data fields required for SNS profiles.

Disconnectors

Those creating and maintaining disconnection can be human and non-human in nature. Human disconnectors are the most obvious: we engage in choosing who not to friend, what not to retweet, who not to share photos with, who not to tag, and when to use backchannels. But non-humans might also hinder SNS usage, and hence connection. Such disconnection can happen directly, via for instance the automated means I discuss in the next section of this chapter. Functions within a given site may also compete with each other for our attention, presenting us with different connective and disconnective possibilities. For example, newsfeeds in applications may function to distract us from updating our profiles or engaging with the profiles of others. Algorithms, may present us with content from people we interact with more often and lead us away from those we do so less often. Desktop and mobile Apps, in particular, may lack the disconnective functionality of their desktop-browser-based counterparts; some participants reported having problems uploading and removing photography via such routes, for instance. The devices we access SNSs with can also affect our attempts at connectivity because of their processing power, storage capacities, connection speeds and input mechanisms. The philosophy of SNSs and formal institutional social media policies, as non-human actors, are important here too as they specify the terms of connection and disconnection of any given space. Content itself may even cause us not to connect as those choosing not to engage with health campaigns interpreted as having no material impact demonstrate. Non-human disconnectors may also have indirect affects. Associations of germs with washroom facilities, and vehicles with legal structures, can affect the extent to which we might engage with SNSs. Power structures of a given society may also deeply affect connective possibilities as I discuss in more detail later in this chapter.

Disconnection mode

The mode by which disconnection occurs can involve varying levels of automation and manual activity. Importantly, modes of disconnection are not necessarily aligned with human or non-human disconnectors. Automated disconnection can, for instance, refer to the use of algorithms which might moderate intensive use of friending functions, the flagging and removal of content deemed inappropriate by the terms and conditions of a given space and restriction by apps on usage due to, for instance, a calculation of the extent of connection a given user might have. Manual disconnection might have its roots in automated functions, for example, whereby an automated share functions such as unmoderated posting capabilities, lead to controversy and defriending activity. Manual disconnection, in its own right, can involve users choosing not to enact particular functions (liking, sharing, retweeting, tagging) and features of a given SNS, engaging in cut and paste connectivity, and not providing complete or accurate personal information. Manual disconnection might also be undertaken by non-human disconnectors where badly designed interfaces lead to features not being accessible or presentable, for example.

Disconnective power

Fundamentally, when I talk of disconnective practice, I am talking of the exercise, or not, of power. In particular, I am referring to the processes of making of action, or not. As I outlined in Chapter 2, and hopefully as you will have seen throughout the text, this power is manifest in a variety of ways. In the terms Lukes (2005) uses, disconnective practice can involve a one-dimensional view of power whereby A has power over B because they have to ability to influence B's actions beyond their own agency. This basic form of power is obvious and explicit. Examples here are rejecting a friend or follower request, the halting of friending attempts by SNSs because too many requests are being made and the implementation of organisational policies that prohibit access to SNSs at work. It may also involve choosing not to read certain content, or as Crawford (2009) has termed it "tuning out". Two-dimensional power is exercised by confining the scope of decision-making to issues deemed to be relatively safe and by creating mechanisms that aim to prohibit the public airing of conflict. This version of power requires the consideration of the questions of control over agendas. Examples of this at work in relation to disconnective practice could include choosing not to retweet certain material on behalf of others, blocking certain people and applications from posting within someone's SNS space, being selective about the linking of SNS accounts, moderating use at work or in public and engaging in temporal cover through historical editing or by holding off on accepting a connection until they have been deemed appropriate. Three-dimensional power is exercised in an attempt to stop conflict from happening in the first place. It is exercised in ways that those subject to it comply without realising they are doing so. Here matters are constructed in ways that appear natural, even though such actions undertaken by those subject to such power might not be in their interests. An example here is where one might refer to narratives regarding the construction of the appropriateness of particular content and action by others in conjunction with SNSs. Here these others are not just users in the typical sense of the word, they are users as developers, users as financial stakeholders in SNSs, users as organisational members of SNS companies. Not only is this situation concerned with what can be said and done by individuals as written into policies of use, it is key here to understand how even things that are not made explicit are enrolled. Here one might refer back to early work on menu-driven identity and how race is written into interfaces (Kolko 2000, Nakamura 2002). In a similar way, one might ask here why it is not possible to create polyamorous connections within Facebook. Why is it okay for men to show their nipples but not women? What I also demonstrate is that disconnective power, like power in general, is something of course that one can exercise and also something that one can be subject to. Moreover, seeking out such power dynamics of disconnective practice affords us a critical network theory as per Mejias (2010). Mejias argues that a critical network theory should interrogate the means by which networks secure their borders against radical otherness (not just that which is non-threatening and readily assimilated). He suggests this involves working through how the network protects itself from paranodes. Paranodes are those conceptual spaces that lie beyond the network; they do not conform to its organising logic. Disconnective practice allows us to understand the mechanisms by which networks are configured through absence. In doing this it inverts our approach to understanding networks, starting not from a given context, but starting from a position of interrogating disconnection in order to understand how a given context has come into being.

Ethics of disconnection

Disconnective practice can also be intimately intertwined with questions of ethics. I demonstrate this throughout the whole text through my arguments and data regarding the difficulty of locating morality within SNSs in terms of who or what is responsible for enacting disconnection that has moral questions attached. It is also demonstrated in relation to the exercise of editorial ethics which seeks to prevent harm to oneself and others through the enactment of selective disconnection. Such work can employ a number of strategies such as those labelled privately public and publicly private by Lange (2007), or the deployment of recontextualisation work and linguistic cover as I have alluded to in this text. Such acts could even be as simple as not posting about someone or not tagging someone in a photograph with an SNS. Questions of how SNSs themselves may cause harm where disconnection does not occur are also raised – people's experiences of uncensored shocking video content for example. Ethical judgements may also be tied to notions of disconnection whereby a person choosing not to connect for a given reason (such as not sharing a serious health condition) is written into being as doing the right thing. Such people might then be compared with those who choose to indulge themselves in self-pity, or the sharing of matters deemed not suitable for public consumption. Judgement may also play into notions of expectations of privacy where, if one has not engaged filters and functions appropriately, one cannot expect others not to interrogate your personal space. The ethics of disconnection is complicated and not easily tied to one strand of philosophical ethics (Johnson 2001, Adam 2005, Ess 2009), and especially to those which are normative in nature. This is because, as my work demonstrates very much, the moral questions people face with SNSs vary in interpretation, importance and impact and are consequently subject to negotiation. Despite the difficulties of establishing an ethics of disconnection, it is an important consideration requiring careful thought before being written out of any analysis of disconnective practice.

What scope for disconnective lenses?

The theory of disconnective practice I have constructed then, acts as a collection of lenses, which allow us to understand who or what is involved, where it occurs and how it is enacted. It also, crucially, sheds light on why such practices might be enrolled. Privacy is perhaps the most obvious reason here, and it is evident throughout the text. However, we also see a series of other things coming into play such as notions of respect, relevance, timing, media overload, fun, a lack of anonymity, a desire for anonymity, and whether we understand our audiences, imagined or otherwise. Disconnection makes connectivity possible. We cannot be connected to everything all the time (even though technologies may stand in for us sometimes (Licoppe and Smoreda 2005)) and therefore we have to disconnect in some way in order to make the connections we want to emphasise at a particular point in time feasible. Moreover, such a lens demonstrates how disconnection is necessarily temporally situated in as much connection is. Disconnective practice, allows a series of options commonly associated with SNSs to be translated into conditions we do not necessarily have to choose between. Disconnective practice, can allow us to choose to be efficient in the management of our relationships, by having all our connections in one place if we wish, alongside being able to attempt to manage such a diverse audience. We can also attempt to strengthen connection and our relationships by selectively aiming to control our presence through, for instance, disconnection via tiering (Dena 2008), and the deployment of redactional acumen (Papacharissi 2010). Finally, disconnective practice can allow us cover, the ability to craft what we might interpret safe spaces in the so-called real name Web. I disagree that "everyone's life is a open book" (Poole 2009). Disconnection then is not merely about resistance to surveillance, or attempting to leave a site, it is also about adding value to our experiences.

A potential area of expansion of this work would be via the consideration of a broader range of cultural contexts and experiences. Mindful of critique of studies of the Internet (Goggin and McLelland 2009), I need to signal the deeply western nature of this text. In doing so I realise I also fall foul of other scholars who have pointed out that acknowledging conceptual specificity should involve more than noting things might be different elsewhere as an afterthought or disclaimer (Paasonen 2009). I know that SNS research has predominantly been driven by a western tradition and this work adds to that. However, I offer small insights into how matters might be elsewhere. I do this through exploring notions of cultures of pet ownership and ethnicity and the potential of networking for Ghanaian funerals in Chapter 7. I agree that by drawing on case studies of SNSs outside western-centric models, we can reflect on the different ways by which the Internet is constituted by various online communities and how this inflects offline forms of locality (Hjorth 2009). For instance, how might the aesthetics of cute (Hjorth 2009) play out as a disconnective device in comparison to its connective potential in South Korea? How might a lack of judgement viz engagement with online gaming affect disconnective practice in this arena?

We know that as terms travel, they are reworked, debated and refined (Paasonen 2009). The question here then is, through my travels with the term SNSs, and given my focus on disconnection, do I believe we need to revise our definitions in order to give us analytical clarity? Indeed, in the introduction to this text and this chapter I have argued that we may need to revisit our ontological and epistemological understandings of SNSs. In some senses then what we believe we can know of SNSs and how we can come to now SNSs surely is tied to how we define them. However, it would be too easy to slot in the words "and disconnection" into existing definitions and be done with it. Moreover, I'm not sure it would be that helpful. As scholars such as danah boyd and Nicole Ellison articulate in their definition, connection is fundamental to SNSs, and whilst I would argue so is disconnection, I would see this more in terms of a necessary function rather than the raison d'être. I am happy therefore, for disconnection to take a backseat when it comes to defining SNSs. What I am more interested in is having disconnection brought to the fore within SNSs research as scholars such as Karppi (2011, 2013, 2014). In social shaping of technology (SST) terms, I would like to see some symmetry in our work.

In terms of moving forward, this work, which started with a focus on mechanisms of engaging with multi-sitedness, and drifted away from it, has in some ways enabled a way of dealing with that. The kind of social formations that I point to are not too dissimilar to those identi-fied by Baym (2007) in her work on the dispersal of Swedish rock fans across various sites of the Internet; she concluded that such formations raise many theoretical, methodological and practical problems of under-standing where they are spread through multiple sites and where they are not explicitly linked to one another. The theoretical framework I pro-pose for interrogating disconnective practice might be one here that could be used in methodological fashion too. It can act as an organ-ising framework setting out potential areas to be probed for evidence of connection *through* disconnection. In effect my participants have told stories of how they craft their own multiple sites in this manner – even within a single site.

In conclusion, I believe that this work adds to our understanding of digitally mediated sociality, responding to Gennaro and Dutton (2007) who have called for a focus on the ways that technology is used and how patterns of use can transform the composition of social networks by reconfiguring networks of communication. In this sense, I see my addition elaborating how patterns of non-use and shades of practices between that and full use might contribute. I also believe this study is one that is comparative in nature and adds to the small but growing body of work on SNSs which crosses platforms (Baym 2007, Baym and Ledbetter 2009, Papacharissi 2009). Through this comparison, with my focus upon disconnection, we are able to see theoretical links. Whilst sites such as Facebook, Fitlads, Flickr, LinkedIn and Twitter clearly dis-play elements of empirical difference, and we have to be careful about how we generalise from any study of an SNS (Hargittai 2007b, Hargittai and Litt 2012) they do share theoretical possibilities. However, I do not see this as a function of a focus on social practice over being artefact centric (Arora 2011). I agree with Arora that artefacts can change rapidly and that sociality can be more persistent. However, it is the recognition of the coming-into-being of arrangements involving the human and the non-human that has more value for me. As Flanagin et al. (2010) suggest, technologies *are* social practices.

Connection clearly is important when it comes to developing understandings of our engagements with SNSs whether this is through our actions to build identity, relationships, enjoy life, gossip, undertake work, make money, improve our health and wellbeing and the many other things with engage with such spaces for. However, I am not convinced that it is always helpful to maintain a focus upon connection. To be clear, and as I said at the beginning of this text, I do not think current research is necessarily ignorant of this situation. Many of those who study the Internet and SNSs are keen to acknowledge the on going work that people put into making SNSs work for them (Light 2007, boyd 2008c, Griffiths and Light 2008, Baym 2010, boyd 2011, Light et al. 2012, Ellison and boyd 2013), and there is discussion of issues which point to disconnection such as that concerned with leaving SNS (Karppi 2014); resistance and non-use (Hargittai 2007b, Light 2007, Hargittai 2012); the need to take account of listening as well as voice (Crawford 2009); the creation of private spaces (Papacharissi 2010); the value of forgetting (Mayer-Schönberger 2011); and the omission of information (Kendall 2007). Indeed, it is not just within academic circles that disconnection with SNSs is being referred to. In 2009, the word "unfriend", defined as "to remove someone as a 'friend' on a social networking site such as Facebook", was selected by the New Oxford American Dictionary as word of the year (Oxford University Press 2009). We know that SNSs are full of contradictions, despite the strong discourses of connectivity we are presented with by their makers. SNSs contain temporal, spatial and cultural gaps and there is no one author in complete control of the narratives they create. Yet at the same time, we are informed that attempting to delete content in networked publics is futile and our definitions of SNSs emphasise connectivity. The participants in my interviews did not use the words disconnection to describe their actions with SNSs that did not involve connection. Yet the participants experienced disconnection everyday whether it was through engaging it themselves or by seeing others doing it. Indeed some, like Rebecca, even noted disconnection as an increasing trend:

> Whereas now, it's Candy Crush, play Candy Crush. It seems to have evolved to be a lot more of that. And the people who do post statuses seem to post, it seems to be the same people posting the same thing. Like 12 times a day! Rather than how it used to be. It used to be people actually posting it, just interesting little snippets. And it was

nice to, you know, to think "ooh, their kids have grown up a bit, I haven't seen them for a while" see pictures. I does still happen, but not as much, yeah.

(Rebecca, school teacher, 35–44)

Maybe I have a naïve and far too optimistic view of the possibilities for disconnection in the context of network publics and the sophisticated algorithms that operate with SNSs, but I would like to think that we still have scope for crafting lives with digital media that do not have to be completely connected. I believe it is necessary that we rebalance our work a little by emphasising disconnection and disconnectivity. I realise this sounds very grand, but we maybe do need to revisit the ontological and epistemological understandings of SNSs that we have. Connection is fundamental to the operation of SNSs and therefore I can understand why our definitions and research attentions have been directed predominantly in this direction. But connection cannot exist without disconnection and therefore I believe it is just as fundamental to our understanding of what SNSs can be and how we make sense of them. The thinking I put forward in this text regarding disconnective practice, I hope, offers one way we might start to do this.

Notes

2   Theorising Technological Appropriation

1. Primary users are those who are intended to interact directly with the technology, they input data, manipulate data and may consume the output; secondary users are those who are not intended to interact directly with the technology but are intended consumers of the output, bystanders are those who are exposed to (primary and secondary user interactions with) a given technology and its outputs, either consciously or subliminally but are not intended to react or respond to this (Ferneley and Light 2008).

4   Shaping Publics

1. Importantly Livia notes that here pseudonyms are not principally a mode of resistance, or indeed a mechanism necessarily to create privacy, although they may have that effect in some circumstances. Ultimately, she argues, they are intended to be seductive.
2. Stephen Fry is a public figure/celebrity known particularly in the UK as popular member of the Twittersphere (he has over six million followers) – see: http://www.stephenfry.com and @stephenfry

References

Abbate, J. (1999). *Inventing the Internet*. Cambridge, MA, MIT Press.

Adam, A. (2005). *Gender, Ethics and Information Technology*. Basingstoke, Palgrave Macmillan.

Ahern, S., D. Eckles, N. Good, S. King, M. Naaman and R. Nair (2007). Over-Exposed? Privacy Patterns and Considerations in Online and Mobile Photo Sharing. *Proceedings of the SIGCHI Conference on Human Factors in Computing Systems*. M. B. Rosson and D. Gilmore. San Jose, CA, Association of Computers and Machinery: 357–366.

Akrich, M. (1992). The De-Scription of Technical Objects. In *Shaping Technology/Building Society: Studies in Sociotechnical Change*. W. E. Bijker and J. Law, Eds. London, MIT Press: 205–224.

Albrechtslund, A. (2012). Socializing the City: Location Sharing and Online Social Networking. In *Internet and Surveillance: The Challenges of Web 2.0 and Social Media*. C. Fuchs, K. Boersma, A. Albrechtslund and M. Sandoval, Eds. New York, Routledge: 187–197.

Arnold, M. (2003). "On the Phenomenology of Technology." *Information and Organization* 13(4): 231–256.

Arora, P. (2011). "Online Social Sites as Virtual Parks: An Investigation into Leisure Online and Offline." *Information Society* 27(2): 113–120.

Arvidsson, A. (2006). "'Quality Singles': Internet Dating and the Work of Fantasy." *New Media and Society* 8(4): 671–691.

Attwood, F. (2007). "No Money Shot? Commerce, Pornography and New Sex Taste Cultures." *Sexualities* 10(4): 441–456.

Bahfen, N. (2009). Modems, Malaysia and Modernity: Characteristics and Policy Challenges in Internet-Led Development. In *Internationalizing Internet Studies: Beyond Anglophone Paradigms*. G. Goggin and M. McLelland, Eds. New York, Routledge: 163–177.

Baker, A. (2012). "The Exchange of Material Culture among Rock Fans in Online Communities." *Information, Communication & Society* 15(4): 519–536.

Barker, V. and H. Ota (2011). "Mixi Diary Versus Facebook Photos: Social Networking Site Use Among Japanese and Caucasian American Females." *Journal of Intercultural Communication Research* 40(1): 39–63.

Barnes, N. D. and F. R. Barnes (2009). "Equipping Your Organization for the Social Networking Game." *Information Management Journal* 43(6): 28–33.

Baughman, L. L. (2010). "Friend Request or Foe? Confirming the Misuse of Internet and Social Networking Sites by Domestic Violence Perpetrators." *Widener Law Journal* 19(3): 933–966.

Baym, N. (2007) "The New Shape of Online Community: The Example of Swedish Independent Music Fandom." *First Monday* 12(8) Accessed 10 January 2008, from http://firstmonday.org/issues/issue12_8/baym/index.html.

Baym, N. K. (2009). "A Call for Grounding in the Face of Blurred Boundaries." *Journal of Computer-Mediated Communication* 14(3): 720–723.

Baym, N. K. (2010). *Personal Connections in the Digital Age*. Cambridge, MA, Polity.

Baym, N. K. and A. Ledbetter (2009). "Tunes that Bind?" *Information, Communication & Society* 12(3): 408–427.

Beck, J. C. and M. Wade (2006). *The Kids are Alright: How the Gamer Generation is Changing the Workplace*. Boston, Harvard Business School Press.

Beer, B. and R. Burrows (2007) "Sociology and, of and in Web 2.0: Some Initial Considerations." *Sociological Research Online* 12(5) Accessed 1 September 2008, from http://www.socresonline.org.uk/12/5/17.html.

Beer, D. (2008). "Social Network(Ing) Sites... Revisiting the Story So Far: A Response to Danah Boyd & Nicole Ellison." *Journal of Computer-Mediated Communication* 13(2): 516–529.

Beer, D. (2009). "Power through the Algorithm? Participatory Web Cultures and the Technological Unconscious." *New Media & Society* 11(6): 985–1002.

Benedictus, L. (2010) "Twitter's Old Hat If You've Used the Notificator – Social Networking, 1935-Style." *The Guardian – Short Cuts Blog* Accessed 10 June 2012, from http://www.theguardian.com/technology/2010/jun/15/the-notificator-precursor-of-twiitter.

Benkler, Y. (2006). *The Wealth of Networks: How Social Production Transforms Markets and Freedom*. New Haven, Yale University Press.

Bennett, W. L. and A. Segerberg (2012). "The Logic of Connective Action." *Information, Communication & Society* 15(5): 739–768.

Berg, A.-J. and M. Lie (1995). "Feminism and Constructivism: Do Artifacts Have Gender?" *Science, Technology, & Human Values* 20(3): 332–351.

Bermejo, F. (2009). "Audience Manufacture in Historical Perspective: From Broadcasting to Google." *New Media & Society* 11(1/2): 133–154.

Bigge, R. (2006) "The Cost of (Anti-)Social Networks: Identity, Agency and Neo-Luddites." *First Monday* 11(12) Accessed 22 November 2007, from http://www.firstmonday.org.

Bijker, W. E. (1987). The Social Construction of Bakelite: Toward a Theory of Invention. In *The Social Construction of Technological Systems*. W. E. Bijker, T. P. Hughes and T. Pinch, Eds. London, The MIT Press: 159–187.

Bijker, W. E. (1994). The Social Construction of Fluorescent Lighting, or How an Artefact was Invented in its Diffusion Stage. In *Shaping Technology/Building Society: Studies in Sociotechnical Change*. W. E. Bijker and J. Law, Eds. Cambridge, MA, MIT Press: 75–104.

Bijker, W. E. (1995). *Of Bicycles, Bakerlites and Bulbs: Towards a Theory of Sociotechnical Change*. Cambridge, MA, MIT Press.

Bijker, W. E., T. P. Hughes and T. Pinch, Eds. (1987). *The Social Construction of Technological Systems*. London, The MIT Press.

Bijker, W. E., T. P. Hughes and T. Pinch (1989). *The Social Construction of Technological Systems: New Directions in the Sociology and History of Technology*. Cambridge, MA, The MIT Press.

Bijker, W. E. and J. Law (1994). *Shaping Technology/Building Society: Studies in Sociotechnical Change*. Cambridge, MA, MIT Press.

Boczkowski, P. J. and L. A. Lievrouw (2008). Bridging STS and Communication Studies: Scholarship on Media and Information Technologies. In *The Handbook of Science and Technology Studies*. E. J. Hackett, O. Amsterdamska, M. Lynch and J. Wajcman, Eds. Cambridge, MA, MIT Press: 949–977.

Bonsu, S. K. and B. DeBerry-Spence (2008). "Consuming the Dead: Identity and Community Building Practices in Death Rituals." *Journal of Contemporary Ethnography* 37(6): 694–719.

boyd, d. (2004a). Friendster and Publicly Articulated Social Networks. *Proceedings of the Conference on Human Factors and Computing Systems – CHI2004*. Vienna, Austria, ACM Press: 1279–1282.

boyd, d. (2008a). "Facebook's Privacy Trainwreck." *Convergence* 14(1): 13–20.

boyd, d. (2008b). *Taken out of Context: American Teen Sociality in Networked Publics (Unpublished PhD Thesis)*. Berkley, CA, University of California-Berkeley.

boyd, d. (2008c). Why Youth ♡ Social Network Sites: The Role of Networked Publics in Teenage Social Life. In *Youth Identity and Digital Media*. D. Buckingham, Ed. Cambridge, MA, MIT Press: 119–142.

boyd, d. (2011). Social Network Sites as Networked Publics. In *A Networked Self: Identity, Community and Culture on Social Network Sites*. Z. Papacharissi, Ed. New York, Routledge: 39–58.

boyd, d. (2012). White Flight in Networked Publics? How Race and Class Shaped American Teen Engagement with Myspace and Facebook. In *Race after the Internet*. L. Nakamura and P. A. Chow-White, Eds. New York, Routledge: 203–222.

boyd, d. m. (2006) "Friends, Friendsters, and Top 8: Writing Community into Being on Social Network Sites." *First Monday* 11(12) Accessed 10 May 2008, from http://firstmonday.org/issues/issue11_12/boyd/index.html.

boyd, d. m. (2008). "Facebook's Privacy Trainwreck." *Convergence: The Journal of Research into New Media Technologies* 14(1): 13–20.

boyd, d. m. and N. B. Ellison (2007). "Social Network Sites: Definition, History, and Scholarship." *Journal of Computer-Mediated Communication* 13(1): 210–230.

Brendryen, H. and P. Kraft (2008). "Happy Ending: A Randomized Controlled Trial of a Digital Multi-Media Smoking Cessation Intervention." *Addiction* 103(3): 478–484.

Brock, T. P. and S. R. Smith (2007). "Using Digital Videos Displayed on Personal Digital Assistants (PDAs) to Enhance Patient Education in Clinical Settings." *International Journal of Medical Informatics* 76(11–12): 829–835.

Brown, V. R. and E. D. Vaughn (2011). "The Writing on the (Facebook) Wall: The Use of Social Networking Sites in Hiring Decisions." *Journal of Business and Psychology* 26(2): 219–225.

Bruns, A. (2008). *Blogs, Wikipedia, Second Life, and Beyond: From Production to Produsage*. New York, Peter Lang.

Bull, S. (2010). *Technology-Based Health Promotion*. Los Angeles, CA, Sage Publications.

Burgess, J. (2014). "From 'Broadcast Yourself' to 'Follow Your Interests': Making over Social Media." *International Journal of Cultural Studies*, Accessed 17 January 2014, Online First Version: http://ics.sagepub.com/content/early/2014/01/13/1367877913513684.abstract..

Burgess, J. and J. Green (2009). *YouTube: Online Video and Pariciparoty Culture*. Cambridge, MA, Polity Press.

Callon, M. (1989). Society in the Making: The Study of Technology as a Tool for Sociological Analysis. In *The Social Construction of Technological Systems: New Directions in the Sociology and History of Technology*. W. E. Bijker, T. P. Hughes and T. Pinch, Eds. Cambridge, MA, The MIT Press: 83–103.

Cant, B. (2004) "Facilitating Social Networks among Gay Men." *Sociological Research Online* 9(4) Accessed 1 September 2008, from http://www.socresonline.org.uk/9/4/cant.html

Carne, E. B. (1979). "The Wired Household: Teletext Services Pave the Way for a Variety of Useful Monitoring and Control Features in the Home." *Spectrum, IEEE* 16(10): 61–66.

Carter, D. (2005). "Living in Virtual Communities: An Ethnography of Human Relationships in Cyberspace." *Information Communication and Society* 8(2): 148–167.

Cassidy, E. (2013). *Gay Men, Social Media and Self-Presentation: Managing Identities in Gaydar, Facebook and Beyond (Unpublished PhD Thesis).* Brisbane, Australia, Queensland University of Technology.

Castells, M. (2004). Informationalism, Networks and the Network Society: A Theoretical Blueprint. In *The Network Society: A Cross-Cultural Perspective.* M. Castells, Ed. Northampton, MA, Edward Elgar Publishing: 3–45.

Chesher, C. (2007). "Becoming the Milky Way: Mobile Phones and Actor Networks at a U2 Concert." *Continuum: Journal of Media & Cultural Studies* 21(2): 217–225.

Clark, L. and S. Roberts (2010). "Employer's Use of Social Networking Sites: A Socially Irresponsible Practice." *Journal of Business Ethics* 95(4): 507–525.

Cohen, K. R. (2005). "What Does the Photoblog Want?" *Media, Culture & Society* 27(6): 883–901.

Constine, J. and G. Ferenstein (2013). "Facebook Doesn't Want to Be Cool, It Wants to Be Electricity." *TechCrunch* Accessed 28 November 2013, from http://techcrunch.com/2013/09/18/facebook-doesnt-want-to-be-cool/.

Cover, R. (2012). "Performing and Undoing Identity Online: Social Networking, Identity Theories and the Incompatibility of Online Profiles and Friendship Regimes." *Convergence: The Journal of Research into New Media Technologies* 18(2): 177–193.

Cox, A. (2007). Flickr: What Is New in Web 2.0? *Towards a Social Science of Web* York, UK, Accessed 10 May 2008. http://citeseerx.ist.psu.edu/viewdoc/download?doi=10.1.1.123.3467&rep=rep1&type=pdf.

Craft, A. (2007). "Sin in Cyber-Eden: Understanding the Metaphysics and Morals of Virtual Worlds." *Ethics and Information Technology* 9(3): 205–217.

Crawford, G. (1987). "Support Networks and Health-Related Change in the Elderly: Theory-Based Nursing Strategies." *Family and Community Health* 10(2): 39–48.

Crawford, G., V. K. Gosling, G. Bagnall and B. Light (2014). "Is There an App for That? A Case Study of the Potentials and Limitations of the Participatory Turn and Networked Publics for Classical Music Audience Engagement." *Information Communication & Society*: Accessed 31 January 2014, Online First Version: http://www.tandfonline.com/doi/abs/10.1080/1369118X.2013.877953.

Crawford, K. (2009). "Following You: Disciplines of Listening in Social Media." *Continuum: Journal of Media & Cultural Studies* 23(4): 525–535.

Cunliffe, D. (2009). The Welsh Language on the Internet: Linguisitic Resistance in the Age of the Network Society. In *Internationalizing Internet Studies: Beyond Anglophone Paradigms.* G. Goggin and M. McLelland, Eds. New York, Routledge: 96–111.

Davies, M. R. and B. A. Lee (2008). "The Legal Implications of Student Use of Social Networking Sites in the Uk and Us: Current Concerns and Lessons for the Future." *Education & the Law* 20(3): 259–288.

Davis, J. (2010). "Architecture of the Personal Interactive Homepage: Constructing the Self through Myspace." *New Media & Society* 12(7): 1103–1119.

Davis, K. (2012). "Tensions of Identity in a Networked Era: Young People's Perspectives on the Risks and Rewards of Online Self-Expression." *New Media & Society* 14(4): 634–651.

de Witte, M. (2001). *Long Live the Dead! Changing Funeral Celebrations in Asante, Ghana.* Amsterdam, Askant Academic Publishers.

de Witte, M. (2003). "Money and Death: Funeral Business in Asante, Ghana." *Africa* 73(4): 531–559.

Debatin, B., J. P. Lovejoy, A.-K. Horn and B. N. Hughes (2009). "Facebook and Online Privacy: Attitudes, Behaviors, and Unintended Consequences." *Journal of Computer-Mediated Communication* 15(1): 83–108.

Dena, C. (2008). "Emerging Participatory Culture Practices." *Convergence: The Journal of Research into New Media Technologies* 14(1): 41–57.

DiMicco, J. M. and R. M. David (2007). Identity Management: Multiple Presentations of Self in Facebook. *The International ACM Conference on Supporting Group Work.* T. Gross and K. Inkpen. Sanibel Island, FL, Association of Computing Machinery: 383–386.

Doheny-Farina, S. (1998). "The Wired Neighborhood." *Yale: University Press* 168: 287–306.

Donath, J. (2007). "Signals in Social Supernets." *Journal of Computer-Mediated Communication* 13(1): 231–251.

Dubrovsky, V., S. Kiesler and B. Sethna (1991). "The Equalization Phenomenon: Status Effects in Computer-Mediated and Face-to-Face Decision-Making Groups." *Human Computer Interaction* 6(2): 119–146.

Dutton, W. H., G. Blank and D. Groselj (2013). *Cultures of the Internet: The Internet in Britain.* Oxford, University of Oxford.

Edison, T. A. (1878). "The Phonograph and its Future." *The North American Review* 126(262): 527–536.

Effah, J. (2011). *Tracing the Emergence and Formation of Small Dot-Coms in an Emerging Digital Economy: An Actor-Network Theory Approach (Unpublished PhD Thesis).* Salford, UK, University of Salford.

Effah, J. (2014). "The Rise and Fall of a Dot-Com Pioneer in a Developing Country." *Journal of Enterprise Information Management* 27(2): 228–239.

Effah, J. and B. Light (2012). *Organizing Death: On the Emergence and Formation of a Ghanian Online Funeral Business (Unpublished Working Paper).* Salford, UK, University of Salford.

Elder, R. W., R. A. Shults, D. A. Sleet, J. L. Nichols, R. S. Thompson, W. Rajab and Task Force on Community Preventive Services (2004). "Effectiveness of Mass Media Campaigns for Reducing Drinking and Driving and Alcohol-Involved Crashes – a Systematic Review." *American Journal of Preventive Medicine* 27(1): 57–65.

Ellison, N. B., B. Steinfield and C. Lampe (2007). "The Benefits of Facebook 'Friends': Exploring the Relationship Between College Students' Use of Online Social Networks and Social Capital." *Journal of Computer-Mediated Communication* 12(4): 1143–1168.

Ellison, N. B., C. Steinfield and C. Lampe (2006). Spatially Bounded Online Social Networks and Social Capital: The Role of Facebook. *Proceedings of the 56th Annual Conference of the International Communication Association*. Dresden, Germany: sic.

Ellison, N. B. and d. boyd (2013). Sociality Through Social Networks. In *The Oxford Handbook of Internet Studies*. W. H. Dutton, Ed. Oxford, Oxford University Press: 151–172.

Ellison, N. B., C. Steinfield and C. Lampe (2011). "Connection Strategies: Social Capital Implications of Facebook-Enabled Communication Practices." *New Media & Society* 13(6): 873–892.

Ess, C. (2009). *Digital Media Ethics*. Cambridge, MA, Polity Press.

Everitt, D. and S. Mills (2009). "Cultural Anxiety 2.0." *Media, Culture & Society* 31(5): 749–768.

Evers, C. W., K. Albury, P. Byron and K. Crawford (2013). "Young People, Social Media, Social Network Sites and Sexual Health Communication in Australia: 'This is Funny, You Should Watch it'." *International Journal of Communication* 7(sic): 263–280.

Eysenbach, G. (2008). Credibility of Health Information and Digital Media: New Perspectives and Implications for Youth. In *Digital Media, Youth, and Credibilty*. M. J. Metzger and A. J. Flanagin, Eds. Cambridge, MA, The MIT Press: 123–154.

Facebook (2014) "Facebook Friending Practice Help Statement." Accessed 1 February 2014, from http://www.facebook.com/help/320587401313728.

Feenberg, A. (1992). From Information to Communication. Videotext. In *Contexts of Computer-Mediated Communication*. M. Lea, Ed. London, Harvester Wheatsheaf: 168–187.

Feenberg, A. (1995). *Alternative Modernity: The Technical Turn in Philosophy and Social Theory*. Berkeley, University of California Press.

Ferneley, E. and B. Light (2006). "Secondary User Relations in Emerging Mobile Computing Environments." *European Journal of Information Systems* 15(3): 301–306.

Ferneley, E. and B. Light (2008). "Unpacking User Relations in an Emerging Ubiquitous Computing Environment: Introducing the Bystander." *Journal of Information Technology* 23(3): 163–175.

Ferreday, D. and S. Lock (2007). Computer Cross-Dressing: Queering the Virtual Subject. In *Queer Online: Media, Technology and Sexuality*. K. O'Riordan and D. Phillips, Eds. New York, Peter Lang: 155–176.

Fiore, A. T. and J. S. Donath (2004). Online Personals: An Overview. *CHI'04 Extended Abstracts on Human Factors in Computing Systems*, Association of Computing Machinery: 1395–1398.

Flanagin, A. J., C. Flanagin and J. Flanagin (2010). "Technical Code and the Social Construction of the Internet." *New Media & Society* 12(2): 179–196.

Fleck, J. (1994). "Learning by Trying: The Implementation of Configurational Technology." *Research Policy* 23(6): 637–652.

Fraser, N. (1990). "Rethinking the Public Sphere: A Contribution to the Critique of Actually Existing Democracy." *Social Text* (25/26): 56–80.

Friedman, A. L. and D. S. Cornford (1989). *Computer Systems Development: History, Organization and Implementation*. Chichester, John Wiley and Sons.

Friend, K. and D. T. Levy (2002). "Reductions in Smoking Prevalence and Cigarette Consumption Associated with Mass-Media Campaigns." *Health Education Research* 17(1): 85–98.

Fuchs, C. (2010). "Class, Knowledge and New Media." *Media, Culture & Society* 32(1): 141–150.

Fuchs, C. (2011). *Foundations of Critical Media and Information Studies.* New York, Routledge.

Galston, W. A. (2000). "Does the Internet Strengthen Community?" *National Civic Review* 89(3): 193–202.

Gane, N., C. Venn and M. Hand (2007). "Ubiquitous Surveillance Interview with Katherine Hayles." *Theory, Culture & Society* 24(7–8): 349–358.

Gehl, R. W. (2011). "The Archive and the Processor: The Internal Logic of Web 2.0." *New Media & Society* 13(8): 1228–1244.

Gennaro, C. D. and W. H. Dutton (2007). "Reconfiguring Friendships: Social Relationships and the Internet." *Information Communication and Society* 10(5): 591–618.

Gerlitz, C. and A. Helmond (2013). "The Like Economy: Social Buttons and the Data-Intensive Web." *New Media & Society* 15(8): 1348–1365.

Goffman, E. (1959). *The Presentation of Self in Everyday Life.* New York, Doubleday.

Goggin, G. (2009). "Adapting the Mobile Phone: The Iphone and its Consumption." *Continuum: Journal of Media & Cultural Studies* 23(2): 231–244.

Goggin, G. and M. McLelland (2009). Internationalizing Internet Studies: Beyond Anglophone Paradigms. In *Internationalizing Internet Studies: Beyond Anglophone Paradigms.* G. Goggin and M. McLelland, Eds. New York, Routledge: 3–17.

Gomez, E. A. (2008). Connecting Communities of Need with Public Health: Can SMS Text-Messaging Improve Outreach Communication? *Proceedings of the 41st Hawaii International Conference on System Sciences – 2008.* Big Island, Hawaii.

Graham, S. (2004). The Software-Sorted City: Rethinking the "Digital Divide". In *The Cybercities Reader.* S. Graham, Ed. London, Routledge: 324–332.

Graham, S. D. (2005). "Software-Sorted Geographies." *Progress in Human Geography* 29(5): 562–580.

Gray, N. J. and J. D. Klein (2006). "Adolescents and the Internet: Health and Sexuality Information." *Current Opinion in Obstetrics and Gynecology* 18(5): 519–524.

Gray, N. J., J. D. Klein, P. R. Noyce, T. S. Sesselberg and J. A. Cantrill (2005a). "Health Information-Seeking Behaviour in Adolescence: The Place of the Internet." *Social Science & Medicine* 60(7): 1467–1478.

Gray, N. J., J. D. Klein, P. R. Noyce, T. S. Sesselberg and J. A. Cantrill (2005b). "The Internet: A Window on Adolescent Health Literacy." *The Journal of Adolescent Health* 37(3): 243–247.

Gregg, M. (2009). "Banal Bohemia Blogging from the Ivory Tower Hot-Desk." *Convergence: The International Journal of Research into New Media Technologies* 15(4): 470–483.

Griffiths, M. and B. Light (2008). "Social Networking and Digital Gaming Media Convergence: Classification and its Consequences for Appropriation." *Information Systems Frontiers* 10(4): 447–459.

Griffiths, R. and S. Casswell (2010). "Intoxigenic Digital Spaces? Youth, Social Networking Sites and Alcohol Marketing." *Drug & Alcohol Review* 29(5): 525–530.

Grimmelmann, J. (2005). "Regulation by Software." *Yale Law Journal* 114(7): 1719–1758.

Gross, R. and A. Acquisti (2005). Information Revelation and Privacy in Online Social Networks. *Proceedings of the 2005 ACM Workshop on Privacy in the Electronic Society.* V. Atluri, S. De Capitani di Vimercati and R. Dingledine. Alexandria, VA, USA, Association of Computing and Machinery: 71–80.

Gye, L. (2007). "Picture This: The Impact of Mobile Camera Phones on Personal Photographic Practices." *Continuum: Journal of Media & Cultural Studies* 21(2): 279–288.

Habermas, J. (1991). *The Structural Transformation of the Public Sphere: An Inquiry into a Category of Bourgeois Society.* Cambridge, MA, MIT press.

Halavais, A. M. C. (2012). "A Genealogy of Badges." *Information, Communication & Society* 15(3): 354–373.

Hampton, K. (2004). Networked Sociability Online, Off-Line. In *The Networked Society: A Cross Cultural Perspective.* M. Castells, Ed. Cheltenham, Edward Elgar Publishing Limited: 217–232.

Hampton, K. and B. Wellman (2001). "Long Distance Community in the Network Society Contact and Support Beyond Netville." *American Behavioral Scientist* 45(3): 476–495.

Hampton, K. N. and N. Gupta (2008). "Community and Social Interaction in the Wireless City: Wi-Fi Use in Public and Semi-Public Spaces." *New Media & Society* 10(6): 831–850.

Hargittai, E. (2007). "Whose Space? Differences among Users and Non-Users of Social Network Sites." *Journal of Computer-Mediated Communication* 13(1): 276–297.

Hargittai, E. (2012). Open Doors, Closed Spaces? Differentiated Adoption of Social Network Sites by User Background. In *Race after the Internet.* L. Nakamura and P. A. Chow-White, Eds. New York, Routledge: 223–245.

Hargittai, E. and Y.P. Hsieh (2011). From Dabblers to Omnivores: A Typology of Social Network Site Usage. In *A Networked Self: Identity, Community and Culture on Social Network Sites.* Z. Papacharissi, Ed. New York, Routledge: 146–168.

Hargittai, E. and E. Litt (2011). "The Tweet Smell of Celebrity Success: Explaining Variation in Twitter Adoption Among a Diverse Group of Young Adults." *New Media & Society* 13(5): 824–842.

Hargittai, E. and E. Litt (2012). "Becoming a Tweep." *Information, Communication & Society* 15(5): 680–702.

Hargittai, E., W. R. Neuman and O. Curry (2012). "Taming the Information Tide: Perceptions of Information Overload in the American Home." *Information Society* 28(3): 161–173.

Hassan, R. (2008). *The Information Society.* Cambridge, MA, Polity.

Haythornthwaite, C. (2000). "Online Personal Networks Size, Composition and Media Use among Distance Learners." *New Media & Society* 2(2): 195–226.

Haythornthwaite, C. (2002). "Strong, Weak, and Latent Ties and the Impact of New Media." *The Information Society* 18(5): 385–401.

Haythornthwaite, C. (2005). "Social Networks and Internet Connectivity Effects." *Information Communication and Society* 8(2): 125–147.

Haythornthwaite, C. and B. Wellman (1998). "Work, Friendship, and Media Use for Information Exchange in a Networked Organization." *Journal of the American Society for Information Science* 49(12): 1101–1114.

Hearn, A. (2008). "Meat, Mask, Burdenprobing the Contours of the Brandedself." *Journal of Consumer Culture* 8(2): 197–217.

Hejlesen, O. K., S. Plougmann, B. M. Ege, O. V. Larsen, T. Bek and D. Cavan (2001). "Using the Internet in Patient-Centred Diabetes Care for Communication, Education, and Decision Support." *Studies in Health Technology and Informatics* (2): 1464–1468.

Hilton, S. and K. Hunt (2010). "Coverage of Jade Goody's Cervical Cancer in UK Newspapers: A Missed Opportunity for Health Promotion?" *BMC Public Health* 10(368): sic.

Hjorth, L. (2007). "Snapshots of Almost Contact: The Rise of Camera Phone Practices and a Case Study in Seoul, Korea." *Continuum: Journal of Media & Cultural Studies* 21(2): 227–238.

Hjorth, L. (2009). Gifts of Presence: A Case Study of a South Korean Virtual Community, Cyworld's Mini-Homphy. In *Internationalizing Internet Studies: Beyond Anglophone Paradigms*. G. Goggin and M. McLelland, Eds. New York, Routledge: 237–251.

Hogan, B. (2010). "The Presentation of Self in the Age of Social Media: Distinguishing Performances and Exhibitions Online." *Bulletin of Science, Technology & Society* 30(6): 377–386.

Hogan, B. (2013). Pseudonyms and the Rise of the Real-Name Web. In *A Companion to New Media Dynamics*. J. Hartley, J. Burgess and A. Bruns, Eds. Hoboken, Wiley: 290–307.

Holin, L. and S. Chuen-Tsai (2011). "The Role of Onlookers in Arcade Gaming: Frame Analysis of Public Behaviours." *Convergence: The Journal of Research into New Media Technologies* 17(2): 125–137.

Howcroft, D. and B. Light (2006). "Reflections on Issues of Power in Packaged Software Selection." *Information Systems Journal* 16(3): 215–235.

Howcroft, D. and B. Light (2010) "The Social Shaping of Packaged Software Selection." *Journal of the Association for Information Systems* 11(3) Accessed 10 January 2011, from http://aisel.aisnet.org/jais/vol11/iss3/2/.

Humphreys, L. (2007). "Mobile Social Networks and Social Practice: A Case Study of Dodgeball." *Journal of Computer-Mediated Communication* 13(1): 341–360.

Hutchby, I. (2001). "Technologies, Texts and Affordances." *Sociology* 35(2): 441–456.

Hutchins, B. and J. Mikosza (2010). "The Web 2.0 Olympics." *Convergence: The Journal of Research into New Media Technologies* 16(3): 279–297.

Introna, L. D. (2007). "Maintaining the Reversibility of Foldings: Making the Ethics (Politics) of Information Technology Visible." *Ethics and Information Technology* 9(1): 11–25.

Ito, K. E. and J. D. Brown (2010). "To Friend or Not to Friend: Using New Media for Adolescent Health Promotion." *North Carolina Medical Journal* 71(4): 367–372.

Ito, M. (2007). Introduction. In *Networked Publics*. K. Varnelis, Ed. London, MIT Press: 1–14.

Jackson, M. H. (1997). "Assessing the Structure of Communication on the World Wide Web." *Journal of Computer-Mediated Communication* 3(1) Accessed 20 January 2010 from http://onlinelibrary.wiley.com/doi/10.1111/j.1083-6101.1997.tb00063.x/abstract.

Jenkins, H. (2008). *Convergence Culture: Where Old and New Media Collide*. New York, New York University Press.

Jenkins, H. (2009). What Happened Before YouTube? In *YouTube: Online Video and Pariciparoty Culture*. J. Burgess and J. Green, Eds. Cambridge, MA, Polity Press: 109–125.

Jernigan, C. and B. F. Mistree (2009) "Gaydar: Facebook Friendships Expose Sexual Orientation." *First Monday* 14(10) Accessed 20 January 2010, from http://www.scopus.com/inward/record.url?eid=2-s2.0-71649097455&partnerID=40&md5=232af0b3151954c97743f26b407dc606.

Johnson, B. (2010) "Privacy No Longer a Social Norm, Says Facebook Founder." *The Guardian* Accessed 28 November 2013, from http://www.theguardian.com/technology/2010/jan/11/facebook-privacy.

Johnson, D. G. (1997). "Ethics Online." *Communications of the ACM* 40(1): 60–65.

Johnson, D. G. (2001). *Computer Ethics*. Upper Saddle River, Prentice Hall.

Joinson, A. N. (2008). Looking at, Looking up or Keeping up with People?: Motives and Use of Facebook. *Proceedings of the Twenty-Sixth Annual SIGCHI Conference on Human Factors in Computing Systems*. M. Czerwinski, A. Lund and D. Tan, Eds. Florence, Italy, Association of Computing Machinery: 1027–1036.

Jones, S. (1997). The Internet and its Social Landscape. In *Virtual Culture: Identity and Communication in Cybersociety*. S. Jones, Ed. London, SAGE Publications Ltd: 7–36.

Jones, S. G. (1995). Understanding Community in the Information Age. In *Cybersociety: Computer Mediated Communication and Community*. S. G. Jones, Ed. Thousand Oaks, Sage: 10–35.

Juarascio, A. S., A. Shoaib and C. A. Timko (2010). "Pro-Eating Disorder Communities on Social Networking Sites: A Content Analysis." *Eating Disorders* 18(5): 393–407.

Kahol, K. (2011). "Integrative Gaming: A Framework for Sustainable Game-Based Diabetes Management." *Journal of Diabetes Science & Technology* 5(2): 293–300.

Kakihara, M., C. Sørensen and M. Wiberg (2002). Fluid Interaction in Mobile Work Practices. *1st Tokyo Mobile Roundtable, Mobile Innovation Research Program*. Institute of Innovation Research, Hitotsubashi University, Tokyo, Japan: sic.

Kaldo, V., S. Levin, J. Widarsson, M. Buhrman, H. C. Larsen and G. Andersson (2008). "Internet Versus Group Cognitive-Behavioral Treatment of Distress Associated with Tinnitus: A Randomized Controlled Trial." *Behavior Therapy* 39(4): 348–359.

Karppi, T. (2011). "Digital Suicide and the Biopolitics of Leaving Facebook." *Transformations – Journal of Media and Culture* (20). Accessed 19 March 2014, from http://www.transformationsjournal.org/journal/issue_20/article_02.shtml

Karppi, T. (2013). " 'Change Name to No One. Like People's Status' Facebook Trolling and Managing Online Personas." *The Fibreculture Journal* (22). Accessed 23 March 2014, from http://twentytwo.fibreculturejournal.org/fcj-166-change-name-to-no-one-like-peoples-status-facebook-trolling-and-manag ing-online-personas/

Karppi, T. (2014). *Disconnect.Me User Engagement and Facebook (Thesis Narrative for PhD by Publication)*. Turku.

Katz, J. E. and P. Aspden (1997). "Motivations for and Barriers to Internet Usage: Results of a National Public Opinion Survey." *Internet Research* 7(3): 170–188.

Kaupins, G. and S. Park (2011). "Legal and Ethical Challenges of Corporate Social Networking." *Journal of Communications Research* 2(2/3): 119–145.

Kelly, M., D. McDaid, A. Ludbrook and J. Powell (2005). *Economic Appraisal of Public Health Interventions*. London, UK, NHS Health Development Agency.

Kendall, L. (2007) " 'Shout into the Wind, and It Shouts Back' Identity and Interactional Tensions on Livejournal" *First Monday* 12(9) Accessed 25 July 2009, from http://firstmonday.org/issues/issue12_9/kendall/index.html.

Kennedy, T. L. M. and B. Wellman (2007). "The Networked Household." *Information Communication and Society* 10(5): 645–670.

Kline, R. and T. Pinch (1996). "Users as Agents of Technological Change: The Social Construction of the Automobile in the Rural United States." *Technology and Culture* 37(4): 763–795.

Kolko, B. E. (2000). Erasing @Race: Going White in the (Inter)Face. In *Race in Cyberspace*. B. E. Kolko, L. Nakamura and G. B. Rodman, Eds. New York, Routledge: 213–232.

Korda, H. and Z. Itani (2013). "Harnessing Social Media for Health Promotion and Behavior Change." *Health Promotion Practice* 14(1): 15–23.

Kraut, R., S. Kiesler, B. Boneva, J. Cummings, V. Helgeson and A. Crawford (2002). "Internet Paradox Revisited." *Journal of Social Issues* 58(1): 49–74.

Kraut, R., M. Patterson, V. Lundmark, S. Kiesler, T. Mukophadhyay and W. Scherlis (1998). "Internet Paradox: A Social Technology That Reduces Social Involvement and Psychological Well-Being?" *American Psychologist* 53(9): 1017.

Lampe, C., N. Ellison, B. and C. Steinfield (2007). A Familar Face(Book): Profile Elements as Signals in an Online Social Network. *Proceedings of the SIGCHI Conference on Human Factors in Computing Systems*. M. B. Rosson and D. Gilmore. San Jose, CA, Association of Computers and Machinery: 435–444.

Lange, P. G. (2007). "Publicly Private and Privately Public: Social Networking on YouTube." *Journal of Computer-Mediated Communication* 13(1): 361–380.

Larsen, M. C. (2007). Understanding Social Networking: On Young People's Construction and Co-Construction of Identity Online. *Paper Presented at the Society for Social Studies of Science (4S) Annual Conference*. Montreal, QC: sic.

Lash, S. (2002). *Critique of Information*, London, Sage.

Latour, B. (1987). *Science in Action: How to Follow Scientists and Engineers Through Society*. Cambridge, MA, Harvard University Press.

Latour, B. (2005). *Reassembling the Social: An Introduction to Actor Network Theory*. Oxford, Oxford University Press.

Lauer, J. (2012). "Surveillance History and the History of New Media: An Evidential Paradigm." *New Media & Society* 14(4): 566–582.

Law, J. (1992). "Notes on the Theory of the Actor-Network: Ordering, Strategy and Heterogeneity." *Systems Practice* 5(4): 379–393.

Lee, D.-H. (2005) "Women's Creation of Camera Phone Culture." *Fibreculture Journal* 6(sic) Accessed 12 November 2013, from http://six.fibreculturejournal.org/fcj-038-womens-creation-of-camera-phone-culture/.

Lee, N. (2013). *Facebook Nation: Total Information Awareness*. Dordrecht, Springer.

Lessig, L. (2006). *Code Version 2.0*. New York, Basic Books.

Licklider, J. C. R. and R. W. Taylor (1968). "The Computer as a Communication Device." *Science & Technology*: 21–31.

Licoppe, C. and Z. Smoreda (2005). "Are Social Networks Technologically Embedded?" *Social Networks* 27(4): 317–335.

Lie, M. and K. H. Sørensen, Eds. (1996). *Making Technology Our Own? Domesticating Technology into Everyday Life*. Oslo, Scandanavian University Press.

Lievrouw, L. A. (2012). "The Next Decade in Internet Time." *Information, Communication & Society* 15(5): 616–638.

Light, B. (2007). "Introducing Masculinity Studies to Information Systems Research: The Case of Gaydar." *European Journal of Information Systems* 16(5): 658–665.

Light, B. (2013). "Networked Masculinities and Social Networking Sites: A Call for the Analysis of Men and Contemporary Digital Media." *Masculinities and Social Change* 2(3): 245–265.

Light, B., G. Fletcher and A. Adam (2008). "Gay Men, Gaydar and the Commodification of Difference." *Information Technology and People* 21(3): 300–314.

Light, B., M. Griffiths and S. Lincoln (2012). " 'Connect and Create': Young People, YouTube and Graffiti Communities." *Continuum: Journal of Media & Cultural Studies* 26(3): 1–13.

Light, B. and K. McGrath (2010). "Ethics and Social Networking Sites: A Disclosive Analysis of Facebook." *Information Technology and People* 23(4): 290–311.

Light, B. and P. Ormandy (2011). *Lesbian, Gay and Bisexual Women in the North West: A Multi-Method Study of Cervical Screening Attitudes, Experiences and Uptake*. Salford, UK, University of Salford.

Light, B. and P. Ormandy (2013). *Digital and Social Media: Impacts and Potentials for Cervical Screening Awareness*. Salford, UK, University of Salford.

Light, B. and E. Wagner (2006). "Integration in ERP Environments: Rhetoric, Realities and Organisational Possibilities." *New Technology, Work and Employment* 21(3): 215–228.

Lindgren, S. and R. Lundström (2011). "Pirate Culture and Hacktivist Mobilization: The Cultural and Social Protocols of #Wikileaks on Twitter." *New Media & Society* 13(6): 999–1018.

Liu, H. (2007. "Social Network Profiles as Taste Performances." *Journal of Computer-Mediated Communication* 13(1): 252–275.

Livia, A. (2002). "Public and Clandestine: Gay Men's Pseudonyms on the French Minitel." *Sexualities* 5(2): 201–217.

Livingstone, S. (2008). "Taking Risky Opportunities in Youthful Content: Teenagers' Use of Social Networking Sites for Intimacy, Privacy and Self-Expression." *New Media and Society* 10(3): 393–411.

Livingstone, S. M., Ed. (2005). *Audiences and Publics: When Cultural Engagement Matters for the Public Sphere: Changing Media, Changing Europe*. Bristol, Intellect Books.

Lovnik, G. (2011). *Networks Without a Cause: A Critique of Social Media*. Cambridge, MA, Polity Press.

Lubben, J. and M. Gironda (1996). Assessing Social Support Networks among Older People in the United States. In *The Social Networks of Older People: A Cross-National Analysis*. H. Litwin, Ed. London, Praeger: 143–161.

Ludlow, P. (1996). *High Noon on the Electronic Frontier: Conceptual Issues in Cyberspace*. Cambridge, MA, MIT Press.

Lukes, S. (1974). *Power: A Radical View*. London, Macmillan.

Lukes, S. (1977). *Essays in Social Theory*. London, Macmillan.

Lukes, S. (2005). *Power: A Radical View*. 2nd edn. London, Palgrave Macmillan.

Mackay, H., C. Carne, P. Beynon-Davies and D. Tudhope (2000). "Reconfiguring the User: Using Rapid Application Development." *Social Studies of Science* 30(5): 737–757.

Mackay, H. and G. Gillespie (1992). "Extending the Social Shaping of Technology Approach: Ideology and Appropriation." *Social Studies of Science* 22(4): 685–716.

MacKenzie, D. and J. Wajcman, Eds. (1985). *The Social Shaping of Technology: How the Refrigerator Got its Hum*. Milton Keynes, Open University Press.

Mackenzie, D. and J. Wajcman, Eds. (1999). *The Social Shaping of Technology*. 2nd. edn. Maidenhead, Open University Press.

Magnet, S. (2007). "Feminist Sexualities, Race and the Internet: An Investigation of Suicidegirls.Com." *New Media and Society* 9(4): 577–602.

Manago, A. M. (2013). "Negotiating a Sexy Masculinity on Social Networking Sites." *Feminism & Psychology* 23(4): 478–497.

Marwick, A. and d. boyd (2011a). "To See and Be Seen: Celebrity Practice on Twitter." *Convergence: The Journal of Research into New Media Technologies* 17(2): 139–158.

Marwick, A. E. and d. boyd (2011b). "I Tweet Honestly, I Tweet Passionately: Twitter Users, Context Collapse, and the Imagined Audience." *New Media & Society* 13(1): 114–133.

Mayer-Schönberger, V. (2011). *Delete: The Virtue of Forgetting in the Digital Age*. Princeton, Princeton University Press.

Mazzucato, V., M. Kabki and L. Smith (2006). "Transnational Migration and the Economy of Funerals: Changing Practices in Ghana." *Development and Change* 37(5): 1047–1072.

McLaughlin, M. L., K. K. Osborne and C. B. Smith (1995). Standards of Conduct on Usenet. In *Cybersociety: Computer-Mediated Communication and Community*. S. Jones, Ed. Thousand Oaks, Sage: 90–111.

Mejias, U. A. (2010). "The Limits of Networks as Models for Organizing the Social." *New Media & Society* 12(4): 603–617.

Mele, C. (1999). Cyberspace and Disadvantaged Communities. In *Communities in Cyberspace: The Internet as a Tool for Collective Action*. M. A. Smith and P. Kollock, Eds. London, Routledge: 290–310.

Mesch, G. and I. Talmud (2006). "The Quality of Online and Offline Relationships: The Role of Multiplexity and Duration of Social Relationships." *The Information Society* 22(3): 137–148.

Middleton, C. A. and W. Cukier (2006). "Is Mobile Email Functional or Dysfunctional? Two Perspectives on Mobile Email Usage." *European Journal of Information Systems* 15(3): 252–260.

Miles, I. and G. Thomas (1995). User Resistance to New Interactive Media: Participants, Processes and Paradigms. In *Resistance to New Technology*. M. Bauer, Ed. Cambridge, MA, Cambridge University Press: 255–276.

Milian, M. (2009) "Why Text Messages are Limited to 160 Characters (Interview with Fredhelm Hillebrand)." *Los Angeles Times* Accessed 11 September 2013, from http://latimesblogs.latimes.com/technology/2009/05/invented-text-messaging.html.

Miller, D. (2011). *Tales from Facebook*. Cambridge, MA, Polity Press.

Miller, V. (2008). "New Media, Networking and Phatic Culture." *Convergence: The International Journal of Research into New Media Technologies* 14(4): 387–400.

Mitchell, W. J. (1995). *City of Bits*. Cambridge, MA, MIT Press.

Mowlabocus, S. (2010). *Gaydar Culture: Gay Men Technology and Embodiment in the Digital Age.* Farnham, Ashgate.

Muñoz, R. F. (2010). "Using Evidence-Based Internet Interventions to Reduce Health Disparities Worldwide." *Journal of Medical Internet Research* 12(5): e60.

Murphy, D. (2013). *Twitter.* Cambridge, MA, Polity.

Murthy, D. (2013). *Twitter: Social Communication in the Twitter Age.* Hoboken, Wiley.

Nakamura, L. (2002). *Cybertypes: Race Ethnicity and Identity on the Internet.* London, Routledge.

Negrine, R. and A. Goodfriend (1988). "Public Perceptions of the New Media: A Survey of British Attitudes." *Media, Culture & Society* 10(3): 303–321.

Nissenbaum, H. (1995). Computing and Accountability. In *Computers, Ethics and Social Values.* D. G. Johnson and H. Nissenbaum, Eds. Englewood Cliffs, Prentice Hall: 526–538.

O'Reilly, T. (2005) "What is Web 2.0?" *OReilly.com* Accessed 27 April 2013, from http://oreilly.com/web2/archive/what-is-web-20.html.

Oudshoorn, N. (1999). "On Masculinities, Technologies and Pain: The Testing of Male Contraceptive Technologies in the Clinic and the Media." *Science, Technology and Human Values* 24(2): 265–290.

Oudshoorn, N. and T. Pinch (2005). How Users and Non-Users Matter. In *How Users Matter: The Co-Construction of Users and Technology (2005 Paperback Edition).* N. Oudshoorn and T. Pinch, Eds. London, MIT Press: 1–25.

Oudshoorn, N., E. Rommes and M. Stienstra (2004). "Configuring the User as Everybody: Gender and Design Cultures in Information and Communication Technologies." *Science, Technology, & Human Values* 29(1): 30–63.

Oxford University Press (2009) "Oxford Word of the Year 2009: Unfriend." *OUP Blog* Accessed 3 January 2014, from https://blog.oup.com/2009/11/unfriend/.

Paasonen, S. (2009). What Cyberspace? Travelling Concepts in Internet Research. In *Internationalizing Internet Studies: Beyond Anglophone Paradigms.* G. Goggin and M. McLelland, Eds. New York, Routledge: 18–31.

Paasonen, S. (2010). "Labors of Love: Netporn, Web 2.0 and the Meanings of Amateurism." *New Media & Society* 12(8): 1297–1312.

Papacharissi, Z. (2002a). "The Presentation of Self in Virtual Life: Characteristics of Personal Home Pages." *Journalism & Mass Communication Quarterly* 79(3): 643–660.

Papacharissi, Z. (2002b). "The Self Online: The Utility of Personal Home Pages." *Journal of Broadcasting & Electronic Media* 46(3): 346–368.

Papacharissi, Z. (2009). "The Virtual Geographies of Social Networks: A Comparative Analysis of Facebook, LinkedIn and ASmallWorld." *New Media & Society* 11(1/2): 199–220.

Papacharissi, Z. (2010). *A Private Sphere.* Cambridge, MA, Polity Press.

Papacharissi, Z. (2011). A Networked Self. In *A Networked Self: Identity, Community and Culture on Social Network Sites.* Z. Papacharissi, Ed. New York, Routledge: 304–318.

Parks, M. R. and L. D. Roberts (1998). " 'Making Moosic': The Development of Personal Relationships on Line and a Comparison to their Off-Line Counterparts." *Journal of Social and Personal Relationships* 15(4): 517–537.

Patchin, J. W. and S. Hinduja (2010). "Trends in Online Social Networking: Adolescent Use of Myspace over Time." *New Media & Society* 12(2): 197–216.

Petersen, S. M. (2008) "Loser Generated Content: From Participation to Exploitation." *First Monday* 13(3) Accessed 20 January 2009, from http://www.firstmonday.org.

Pfaffenberger, B. (1992). "Technological Dramas." *Science, Technology and Human Values* 29(1): 30–63.

Pinch, T. (2005). Giving Birth to New Users: How the Minimoog was Sold to Rock and Roll. In *How Users Matter: The Co-Construction of Users and Technology (2005 Paperback Edition)*. N. Oudshoorn and T. Pinch, Eds. London, MIT Press: 247–270.

Pinch, T. and W. Bijker (1986). "Science, Relativism and the New Sociology of Technology: Reply to Russell." *Social Studies of Science* 16(2): 347–360.

Pinch, T. and W. E. Bijker (1984). "The Social Construction of Facts and Artifacts." *Social Studies of Science* 14: 399–441.

Poole, M. S. (2009). "Collaboration, Integration, and Transformation: Directions for Research on Communication and Information Technologies." *Journal of Computer-Mediated Communication* 14(3): 758–763.

Portwood-Stacer, L. (2013). "Media Refusal and Conspicuous Non-Consumption: The Performative and Political Dimensions of Facebook Abstention." *New Media & Society* 15(7): 1041–1057.

Postigo, H. (2008). "Video Game Appropriation Through Modifications." *Convergence: The Journal of Research into New Media Technologies* 14(1): 59–74.

Quan-Haase, A., B. Wellman, J. Witte and K. Hampton (2002). Capitalizing on the Internet: Network Capital, Participatory Capital, and Sense of Community. In *The Internet in Everyday Life*. B. Wellman and C. Haythornthwaite, Eds. Oxford, Blackwell: 291–324.

Raftopoulou, C. (2007). *Audience Reception of Health-Promoting Advertising: Young Adult Smokers Make-Sense, Interpret and Decode Shocking Anti-Smoking Advertisements (Unpublished Thesis)*. London, UK, London School of Economics.

Ralph, L. J., N. F. Berglas, S. L. Schwartz and C. D. Brindis (2011). "Finding Teens in Theirspace: Using Social Networking Sites to Connect Youth to Sexual Health Services." *Sexuality Research and Social Policy* 8(1): 38–49.

Rheingold, H. (1994). *The Virtual Community: Homesteading on the Electronic Frontier*. New York, Harper Perennial.

Rice, E., E. Tulbert, J. Cederbaum, A. Barman Adhikari and N. G. Milburn (2012). "Mobilizing Homeless Youth for HIV Prevention: A Social Network Analysis of the Acceptability of a Face-to-Face and Online Social Networking Intervention." *Health Education Research* 27(2): 226–236.

Rice, R. E. (2006). "Influences, Usage, and Outcomes of Internet Health Information Searching: Multivariate Results from the Pew Surveys." *International Journal of Medical Informatics* 75(1): 8–28.

Rice, R. E. and G. Love (1987). "Electronic Emotion Socioemotional Content in a Computer-Mediated Communication Network." *Communication Research* 14(1): 85–108.

Richardson, K. and S. Hessey (2009). "Archiving the Self? Facebook as Biography of Social and Relational Memory." *Journal of Information, Communication, Ethics and Society* 7(1): 25–38.

Rini, C., D. A. Williams, J. E. Broderick and F. J. Keefe (2012). "Meeting Them Where They Are: Using the Internet to Deliver Behavioral Medicine Interventions for Pain." *Translational Behavioral Medicine* 2(1): 82–92.

Riper, H., V. Spek, B. Boon, B. Conijn, J. Kramer, K. Martin-Abello and F. Smit (2011). "Effectiveness of E-Self-Help Interventions for Curbing Adult Problem Drinking: A Meta-Analysis." *Journal of Medical Internet Research* 13(2): e42.

Robards, B. (2012). "Leaving Myspace, Joining Facebook: 'Growing Up' on Social Network Sites." *Continuum: Journal of Media & Cultural Studies* 26(3): 385–398.

Robinson, J. P., M. Kestnbaum, A. Neustadtl and A. Alvarez (2000). "Mass Media Use and Social Life among Internet Users." *Social Science Computer Review* 18(4): 490–501.

Roharcher, H. (2005). The Diverse Role of Users in Innovation Processes. In *User Involvement in Innovation Processes: Strategies and Limitations from a Socio-Technical Perspective*. H. Roharcher, Ed. Wien, Profil: 9–35.

Röhle, T. (2007). "Desperately Seeking the Consumer: Personalized Search Engines and the Commercial Exploitation of User Data." *First Monday* 12(9) http://firstmonday.org/issues/issue12_19/rohle/index.html.

Russell, D. M., N. A. Streitz and T. Winograd (2005). "Building Disappearing Computers." *Communications of the ACM* 48(3): 42–48.

Russell, S. (1986). "The Social Construction of Artefacts: A Response to Pinch and Bijker." *Social Studies of Science* 16(2): 331–346.

Russell, S. and R. Williams (2002). Social Shaping of Technology: Frameworks, Findings and Implications for Policy with Glossary of Social Shaping Concepts. In *Shaping Technology, Guiding Policy: Concepts, Spaces and Tools*. K. H. SØrensen and R. Williams, Eds. Cheltenham, Edward Elgar: 37–131.

Sauter, T. (2013). " 'What's on Your Mind?' Writing on Facebook as a Tool for Self-Formation." *New Media & Society*: Online First Version: Accessed 1 August 2013, http://nms.sagepub.com/content/early/2013/07/05/1461444813495160.abstract

Schiller, D. (2000). *Digital Capitalism: Networking the Global Market Systems*. Cambridge, MA, MIT Press.

Schmitz, J. and J. Fulk (1991). "Organizational Colleagues, Media Richness, and Electronic Mail a Test of the Social Influence Model of Technology Use." *Communication Research* 18(4): 487–523.

Schwarz, O. (2010). "On Friendship, Boobs and the Logic of the Catalogue." *Convergence: The Journal of Research into New Media Technologies* 16(2): 163–183.

Seeman, T. E. (1996). "Social Ties and Health: The Benefits of Social Integration." *Annals of Epidemiology* 6(5): 442–451.

Sennett, R. (1978). *The Fall of Public Man: On the Social Psychology of Capitalism*. New York, W. W. Norton & Company.

Siegel, M. and L. Biener (2000). "The Impact of an Antismoking Media Campaign on Progression to Established Smoking: Results of a Longitudinal Youth Study." *American Journal of Public Health* 90(3): 380–386.

Silverstone, R. (1996). Future Imperfect: Information and Communication Technologies in Everyday Life. In *Information and Communication Technologies: Visions and Realities*. W. H. Dutton, Ed. Oxford, Oxford University Press: 217–231.

Silverstone, R. (2006). Domesticating Domestication: Reflections on the Life of a Concept. In *The Domestication of Media and Technology*. T. Beker, M. Hartman, Y. Punnie and K. J. Ward, Eds. Maidenhead, Open University Press: 229–248.

Silverstone, R. and E. Hirsch, Eds. (1992). *Consuming Technologies: Media and Information in Domestic Spaces*. London, Routledge.

Silverstone, R., E. Hirsch and D. Morley (1992). Information and Communication Technologies and the Moral Economy of the Household. In *Consuming Technologies: Media and Information in Domestic Spaces*. R. Silverstone and E. Hirsch, Eds. London, Routledge: 15–31.

Skovholt, K. and J. Svennevig (2006). "Email Copies in Workplace Interaction." *Journal of Computer-Mediated Communication* 12(1): 42–65.

Smith, W. P. and D. L. Kidder (2010). "You've been Tagged! (Then Again, Maybe Not): Employers and Facebook." *Business Horizons* 53(5): 491–499.

Söderström, S. (2009). "Offline Social Ties and Online Use of Computers: A Study of Disabled Youth and their Use of Ict Advances." *New Media & Society* 11(5): 709–727.

Song, F. W. (2010). "Theorizing Web 2.0." *Information, Communication & Society* 13(2): 249–275.

Sørensen, K. H. (2002). Social Shaping on the Move? On the Policy Relevance of the Social Shaping of Technology Perspective. In *Shaping Technology, Guiding Policy: Concepts, Spaces and Tools*. K. H. Sørensen and R. Williams, Eds. Cheltenham, Edward Elgar: 19–35.

Sproull, L. S. and S. Kiesler (1992). *Connections: New Ways of Working in the Networked Organization*. Cambridge, The MIT Press.

Stewart, J. (2007). "Local Experts in the Domestication of Information and Communication Technologies." *Information, Communication & Society* 10(4): 547–569.

Stewart, J. and R. Williams (2005). The Wrong Trousers? Beyond the Design Fallacy. In *User Involvement in Innovation Processes: Strategies and Limitations from a Socio-Technical Perspective*. H. Roharcher, Ed. Wien, Profil: 39–71.

Strecher, V. (2007). "Internet Methods for Delivering Behavioral and Health-Related Interventions (Ehealth)." *Annual Review of Clinical Psychology* 3: 53–76.

Subrahmanyam, K., P. M. Greenfield and B. Tynes (2004). "Constructing Sexuality and Identity in an Online Teen Chatroom." *Journal of Applied Developmental Psychology* 25: 651–666.

Sweney, M. (2013a) "Lord Mcalpine Libel Row with Sally Bercow Formally Settled in High Court." *The Guardian* Accessed 23 November 2013, from http://www.theguardian.com/uk-news/2013/oct/22/lord-mcalpine-libel-row-sally-bercow.

Sweney, M. (2013b) "Lord Mcalpine Settles Libel Action with Alan Davies over Twitter Comment." *The Guardian* Accessed 23 November 2013, from http://www.theguardian.com/media/2013/oct/24/lord-mcalpine-libel-alan-davies.

Sweney, M. (2013c) "Newsnight and This Morning Rapped over Lord Mcalpine Claims." *The Guardian* Accessed 23 November 2013, from http://www.theguardian.com/media/2013/oct/23/newsnight-this-morning-lord-mcalpine.

Tierney, T. (2013). *The Public Space of Social Media*. New York, Routledge.

Tiller, J. M., G. Sloane, U. Schmidt, N. Troop, M. Power and J. L. Treasure (1997). "Social Support in Patients with Anorexia Nervosa and Bulimia Nervosa." *International Journal of Eating Disorders* 21(1): 31–38.

Tolson, A. (2010). "A New Authenticity? Communicative Practices on YouTube." *Critical Discourse Studies* 7(4): 277–289.

Tufekcki, Z. (2008). "Grooming, Gossip, Facebook and Myspace: What Can We Learn About These Sites from Those Who Won't Assimilate?" *Information Communication and Society* 11(4): 544–564.

Turner-McGrievy, G. M., M. K. Campbell, D. F. Tate, K. P. Truesdale, J. M. Bowling and L. Crosby (2009). "Pounds Off Digitally Study. A Randomized Podcasting Weight-Loss Intervention." *American Journal of Preventive Medicine* 37(4): 263–269.

Turkle, S. (1995). *Life on the Screen*, London: Weidenfeld & Nicolson.

Valenzuela, J. I., A. Arguello, J. G. Cendales and C. A. Rizo (2007). "Web-Based Asynchronous Teleconsulting for Consumers in Colombia: A Case Study." *Journal of Medical Internet Research* 9(4): e33.

van Dijck, J. (2013a). *The Culture of Connectivity: A Critical History of Social Media*. Oxford, Oxford University Press.

van Dijck, J. (2013b). "Facebook and the Engineering of Connectivity a Multi-Layered Approach to Social Media Platforms." *Convergence: The International Journal of Research into New Media Technologies* 19(2): 141–155.

van Dijck, J. (2013c). " 'You Have One Identity': Performing the Self on Facebook and LinkedIn." *Media, Culture & Society* 35(2): 199–215.

van Dijck, J. and T. Poell (2013). "Understanding Social Media Logic." *Media and Communication* 1(1): 2–14.

van Doorn, N. (2010). "The Ties That Bind: The Networked Performance of Gender, Sexuality and Friendship on Myspace." *New Media & Society* 12(4): 583–602.

van Hoye, G., E. A. J. van Hooft and F. Lievens (2009). "Networking as a Job Search Behaviour: A Social Network Perspective." *Journal of Occupational & Organizational Psychology* 82(3): 661–682.

Viswanath, K. and M. W. Kreuter (2007). "Health Disparities, Communication Inequalities, and Ehealth." *American Journal of Preventive Medicine* 32(5 SUPPL.): S131–S133.

Wajcman, J. (1991). *Feminism Confronts Technology*. Oxford, Polity Press.

Walther, J. B. (1992). "Interpersonal Effects in Computer-Mediated Interaction a Relational Perspective." *Communication Research* 19(1): 52–90.

Waskul, D. and M. Douglas (1997). "Cyberself: The Emergence of Self in on-Line Chat." *The Information Society* 13(4): 375–397.

Wasserman, S. and K. Faust (1994). *Social Network Analysis*. Cambridge, MA, Cambridge University Press.

Weiser, M. (1991). "The Computer of the 21st Century." *Scientific America* 265(3): 94–104.

Weiser, M. and J. S. Brown (1997). The Coming Age of Calm Technology. In *Beyond Calculation: The Next Fifty Years of Computing*. P. Denning and R. Metcalfe, Eds. New York, Springer-Verlag.

Weiser, M., R. Gold and J. S. Brown (1999). "The Origins of Ubiquitous Computing Research at Parc in the Late 1980s." *IBM Systems Journal* 38(4): 693–696.

Weiss, R. and C. P. Samenow (2010). "Smart Phones, Social Networking, Sexting and Problematic Sexual Behaviors-a Call for Research." *Sexual Addiction & Compulsivity* 17(4): 241–246.

Wellings, K. and W. Macdowall (2000). "Evaluating Mass Media Approaches to Health Promotion: A Review of Methods." *Health Education* 100(1): 23–32.

Wellman, B. (1996). "Are Personal Communities Local? A Dumptarian Consideration." *Social Networks* 18(4): 347–354.

Wellman, B. (2001). "Physical Place and Cyberplace: The Rise of Personalized Networking." *International Journal of Urban and Regional Research* 25(2): 227–252.

Wellman, B. and M. Gulia (1999). Net Surfers Don't Ride Alone: Virtual Communities as Communities. In *Communities in Cyberspace*. P. Kollock and M. Smith, Eds. London, Routledge: 331–367.

Wellman, B., A. Q. Haase, J. Witte and K. Hampton (2001). "Does the Internet Increase, Decrease, or Supplement Social Capital?: Social Networks, Participation, and Community Commitment." *American Behavioral Scientist* 45(3): 436–455.

Winner, L. (1999). Do Artifacts Have Politics? In *The Social Shaping of Technology*. D. Mackenzie and J. Wajcman, Eds. Maidenhead, Open University Press: 28–40.

Wittel, A. (2001). "Toward a Network Sociality." *Theory, Culture and Society* 18(6): 51–76.

Wolfendale, J. (2007). "My Avatar, My Self: Virtual Harm and Attachment." *Ethics and Information Technology* 9(2): 111–119.

Woolgar, S. (1991). Configuring the User: The Case of Usability Trials. In *A Sociology of Monsters: Essays on Power, Technology and Domination*. J. Law, Ed. London, Routledge: 66–75.

Wyatt, S. (2005). Non-Users Also Matter: The Construction of Users and Non-Users of the Internet. In *How Users Matter: The Co-Construction of Users and Technology*. N. Oudshoorn and T. Pinch, Eds. London, MIT Press: 67–79.

Wyatt, S., G. Thomas and T. Terranova (2002). They Came, They Surfed, They Went Back to the Beach: Conceptualising Use and Non-Use of the Internet. In *Virtual Society?* S. Woolgar, Ed. Oxford, Oxford University Press: 23–40.

Young, S. (2011). "Television Studies After TV: Understanding Television in the Post-Broadcast Era." *Continuum: Journal of Media & Cultural Studies* 25(1): 125–129.

Zuckerberg, M. (2012) "Form S-1 Registration Statement: Letter from Mark Zuckerberg." *United States Securities and Exchange Commission* Accessed 11 November 2013, from http://www.sec.gov/Archives/edgar/data/1326801/000119312512034517/d287954ds1.htm.

Index